THE COMMUNIST
OF LONI

D1648135

THE
COMMUNIST UNIVERSITY
OF LONDON

Papers on

CLASS, HEGEMONY AND PARTY

edited by JON BLOOMFIELD

1977
LAWRENCE AND WISHART
LONDON

These papers were originally
delivered at the Communist University,
held in London in 1976.

Printed in Great Britain by
The Camelot Press Ltd, Southampton

CONTENTS

PREFACE

JON BLOOMFIELD

Not long ago politicians, academics and intellectuals, newspaper editors and media pundits were all declaring that class conflict was over. We were entering the post-capitalist era free from class struggle – and they weren't meaning communism! In the phrase of one of their foremost spokesmen, Daniel Bell, we had seen 'the end of ideology'. Marxism was no more than a historic curiosity or an anachronistic dogma.

Today its enemies as well as its friends recognize the tremendous power, attraction and resilience of Marxist theory. In Britain the last decade has seen a major renewal of interest in all aspects of Marxism. The central works of classic Marxism are being more and more widely read. British Marxists' contributions, notably in the fields of history and economics, are now being reinforced and developed by a growing band eager to analyse specific aspects of our society, economy, culture and intellectual tradition; and a whole stream of books by Marxists like Antonio Gramsci, Louis Althusser, Karl Korsch, Georg Lukács and Nicos Poulantzas have been translated for the first time.

The shattering of the post-war capitalist boom has had a major effect here. Throughout Europe the late 1960s saw mounting class struggles, with the working class engaged in major battles in France and Italy, and the anti-imperialist and student movements generating new dimensions to popular struggles. In Britain the wide-scale working-class upsurge against the Heath Government, combined with emerging movements among women, students and in the communities, created new conditions more favourable to Marxist theory and socialist politics. At the same time, the development of the process of *détente* eased the ideological straitjacket so characteristic of the Cold War period and gave more breathing space, so to speak, for Marxist ideas. These two factors have been reinforced by a third, the regeneration of Marxism itself, gradually rejecting the deformations of the Stalin period and attempting to analyse the concrete reality of the modern world. This project has not been an easy one, nor is it completed, yet its occurrence bears testimony to the vitality of Marxism as a science rather than a dogma.

Encouraging though these developments are, the reality of Britain today is still of a society where Marxist ideas exert no massive influence at a political level. Despite its militant traditions and struggles the British labour and progressive movement remains bound within a reformist framework, often exhibiting suspicion and hostility to theory in general and Marxism in particular. Yet the events of the last few years confirm that 'militancy is not enough'. This makes the need for Marxist ideas to become widely known, accepted and understood ever more crucial. This is of relevance not just to the working-class movement but also to the emerging, popular movements, for otherwise they will fall prey to their own distinctive forms of sectionalism.

Within the Party's strategy British Communists outline the perspective of a broad, popular alliance drawing together these class and social forces and creating a political majority for democratic advance opening the road to socialism. To further this alliance is both a political and ideological task.

In the last few years, partly in response to more favourable conditions, the Communist Party has increased its programme of public Marxist education. This activity has taken diverse forms corresponding to specific needs. Marxist festivals have been organized in Birmingham, Glasgow, Leeds, Manchester and Sheffield aimed at the broad labour and progressive movement; material has been produced and schools held on the question of women's oppression and liberation; weekend conferences have been arranged for specialists in the fields of sociology, history and literature.

The Communist University of London (CUL) has been a major and very successful development. Its specific role has been to help students to counter the orthodox bourgeois theories they are presented with on their courses and to outline Marxist approaches in the field. As such, it has attracted a wide spectrum of students, along with researchers and young lecturers. From steady beginnings with 160 at CUL 1 in 1969 the attendance has grown considerably with 282 at CUL 5, 632 at CUL 6 and over 1,000 at CUL 8. With this increase has come both a quantitative and qualitative expansion of the university. The core of the 9-day event has remained the 8-session specialist courses. These have not only increased in number so as to cover most subject areas, ranging from literature to science, from sociology to architecture and planning, but have gained in coherence as the Marxist challenge to bourgeois ideology in these disciplines has itself developed. Indeed, the selection of papers we print here deal largely with aspects of Marxist theory and developments within it.

In addition to the specialist courses, the CUL contains a set of general courses. These cover certain themes central to Marxism, e.g. political economy, philosophy, and also analyse major political developments and revolutionary strategies, e.g. women's liberation, strategies in Western Europe, theory of the revolutionary party. Following frequent calls to cover topics not encompassed by strict subject divisions in the past two years, one day has been set aside to discuss 'inter-disciplinary' themes. As well as this, an array of cultural and social events and political discussions are arranged for the evening, ensuring that the CUL is a many-sided event and not a dry, academic exercise.

Three factors have been central to the growing impact of the CUL and the enthusiastic response of many of its participants. Firstly, it has recognized the specific needs of students in their subjects by making the specialist courses the core of the university. Thus while many non-students have taken part, benefited and contributed to the CUL, its emphasis lies with existing students. Secondly, the CUL has refused to lay down a line in the theoretical field. We have followed the position adopted by our party in its document 'On Ideology and Culture' (1967). We do not set ourselves up as an adjudicator on these questions, although clearly the character of the Communist University is informed by our political approach. Thirdly, the involvement as participants and lecturers of many non-Communists, including growing numbers of Labour Party members, combined with the open, workshop atmosphere have helped to guarantee lively but friendly discussions.

So great has been the success of the CUL that provincial weekend mini-universities are being held in several centres, while the activities of our specialist groups have received a considerable boost. It is with a view to making this developing Marxist trend in the academic sphere more powerful that we have decided to publish this selection of papers. They do not – indeed they could not – represent the diverse character of the talks given at the CUL. Rather they tend to concentrate on aspects of Marxism and areas of debate within it. A range of criteria has been deployed in the selection of these papers: interest; originality; contribution to a current controversy, etc. As an editorial collective we have not sought to impose a uniform theoretical line on the material, although we have tried to obtain a selection that will be stimulating and elucidating to all those interested in developing Marxist theory in these areas. We hope we have been successful and that an annual publication of CUL Papers will be possible.

Such a venture, like the CUL itself, aims at contributing to the emergence of Marxism as a growing theoretical force in Britain. For socialism cannot be brought about unless Marxist theory and ideas acquire a new breadth and attraction to tens of thousands of working people, women, intellectuals and students, informing their actions and struggles. In its diverse educational activities the Communist Party seeks to contribute to this process.

Editorial Committee on behalf of CUL

JON BLOOMFIELD
DAVE COUTINHO
ALAN HUNT
JAMES KLUGMANN

THE CONTRIBUTORS

JON BLOOMFIELD studied history at Cambridge and then obtained a Ph.D. with a thesis on the Czechoslovak labour movement in the immediate post-war years. Actively involved in student politics, he became the Communist Party's national student organizer in September 1974. In January 1977 he took over responsibility for the Communist Party's work in Birmingham.

RICHARD GUNN graduated in philosophy at Edinburgh in 1971, and subsequently undertook post-graduate work on the philosophy of Karl Marx. He is currently teaching political theory in the Department of Politics, University of Edinburgh.

STUART HALL was born in Kingston, Jamaica, and was educated there and at Merton College, Oxford. He was one of the founder-editors in 1956 of *Universities and Left Review* and the first editor of *New Left Review*. After working as schoolteacher and university extension lecturer, he became lecturer in media at Chelsea College of Science, London University. Since 1964 he has been Research Fellow of the Centre for Cultural Studies, University of Birmingham, of which he is now the Director.

ROBERT GRAY, born in 1945, studied at the universities of Cambridge and Edinburgh, and now lectures at Portsmouth Polytechnic. He is author of *The Labour Aristocracy in Victorian Edinburgh* and of various articles on class relations in nineteenth-century Britain.

BARRY HINDESS is Senior Lecturer in Sociology at the University of Liverpool. He has served on the editorial boards of *Economy and Society* and *Theoretical Practice*, is the author of *The Decline of Working Class Politics*, *The Use of Official Statistics in Sociology*, and *Philosophy and Methodology in the Social Sciences*, and co-author (with Paul Hirst) of *Pre-capitalist Modes of Production* and *Mode of Production and Social Formation*.

GERRY LEVERSHA studied mathematics at Cambridge. He now lives in Manchester and has recently completed a doctoral research thesis in Logic.

THE COMMUNIST UNIVERSITY
OF LONDON

MARXISM AND IDEAS OF POWER AND PARTICIPATION

RICHARD GUNN

The importance of socialist democracy has, recently, received renewed emphasis within the communist movement. For example, Gordon McLennan's speech as British fraternal delegate at the 25th Congress of the Communist Party of the Soviet Union contained the following succinct statement of the position taken by the British Communist Party:

> Our aim is the construction of socialism in Britain in forms which would guarantee political freedom, the plurality of political parties, the independence of the trade unions, religious freedom and freedom of research, cultural, artistic and scientific activities.

I want to discuss some of the theoretical problems connected with very salutary insistence on the democratic character of socialism. This can only be done, I suggest, by developing a Marxist political theory. In socialist society popular involvement in debating and deciding all matters concerning society as a whole must have a central place; and a crucial step in establishing a Marxist political theory must be the constitution, in Marxist terms, of a conception of the 'political' which recognizes such participation as fundamental. My argument is that such a conception of the political is intrinsic to Marxism.

For this purpose it is useful to examine some issues raised by three writers: Sheldon S. Wolin, Hannah Arendt and Jürgen Habermas. A common concern of these writers is with the 'political' as an authentic dimension of existence where discussion takes place on the goals, purposes and direction of public life. An additional reason for considering Hannah Arendt and Jürgen Habermas is that each of them in the course of developing their position gives an interesting critical discussion of Marx. Habermas is indeed the major current exponent of 'critical theory' as developed by the Frankfurt School (Horkheimer, Adorno, Marcuse *et al.*) and, although we shall take issue with his treatment of Marx, he can with justice see himself as building on some of Marx's most fertile insights.

'The sense of the political', 'the public sphere'

A central theme of Sheldon S. Wolin's major treatment of the tradition of political theory, *Politics and Vision,* is that in the modern world 'the sense of the political has been lost'; 'the contemporary vision of the social universe is one where political society, in its *general* sense, has disappeared'.[1] 'Politics' for Wolin is a form of activity which *inter alia* centres around 'the quest for competitive advantage between groups, individuals or societies'; it is 'both a source of conflict and a mode of activity that seeks to resolve conflicts and promote readjustment'.[2] The general theme announced by Wolin of the 'political' and its fate can be pursued by looking at a related concept which plays an important role in the writings of Habermas: that of the 'public sphere'. Indeed Wolin's comments on the political find a precise parallel in Habermas's observations on 'the decline of the public realm as a political institution'.[3]

Habermas defines the public sphere as 'a realm of our social life in which something approaching public opinion can be formed'. It is the sphere of 'public discussion' on 'matters of general interest'; and we may speak, he says, of the 'political public sphere' when such discussion 'deals with objects connected to the activity of the state'. (The political public sphere is, however, 'not a part' of the state but, rather, 'mediates between society and the state'.) A public sphere presupposes the 'democratic' condition that information is generally accessible and hence, 'in a large public body', means of communication such as the press. Habermas considers that a public sphere came into existence with the rise of the liberal bourgeoisie in the eighteenth century and that currently there is a 'trend towards the weakening of the public sphere as a principle'. There are, he indicates, counter-tendencies to this 'weakening' – but these remain obscure.[4]

Turning to Hannah Arendt we may note, first, that the concept of the public sphere is one with deep philosophical roots. This emerges from her account of it as a 'space of appearances',[5] a political space in which the human agent is revealed to others and gains human recognition from them above all through the medium of 'speech'.[6] The 'Aristotelianism' of this view will be noted below.

Like Wolin and Habermas, Arendt believes that the modern world sees 'the withering of the public realm': 'Society,' she tells us, 'has conquered the public realm'.[7] Common to the three writers is the view that the 'political' has lost its specificity as a general dimension of existence, that in place of participation, real debate and 'critical analysis of the quality, direction or fate of public life'[8] there is a technical, supposedly value-neutral concern with efficiency and security: with 'life' rather than 'good life' and with 'pleasure' rather than 'happiness'.

In this context Wolin develops a conception of political theory which runs parallel to the conception of critical theory articulated by the Frankfurt School: the vocation of political theory is the defence and reconstitution of the political. Habermas's public sphere is, indeed, the sphere of critical consciousness and to the extent that it is eroded social consciousness sinks into technocracy or, in Marcuse's phrase, becomes one-dimensional. In this line of thought – the championing of the 'political' against the 'technical' – there is an evident danger of slipping into a purely romantic protest against the technical as such. I shall suggest that Habermas is alive to this danger and successfully avoids it; the same, however, cannot be said of Marcuse.[9]

Some further exposition is necessary to set the scene for discussion. In both Arendt and Habermas the treatment of the public sphere is situated within a conceptual structure which relates politics (participation in the political public sphere) to other modalities of human practice. In *The Human Condition* Arendt's concern is with the articulations internal to what, following tradition, she calls the *vita activa*.

She draws a threefold distinction between what she terms 'labour', 'work' and 'action'. *Labour* is in Arendt's definition 'the activity which provides the means of consumption'. It is a function of the metabolism or interchange with nature which man must sustain in order for life to be possible and as such 'always moves in the same circle, which is prescribed by the biological process of the living organisms' (*HC*, pp. 98–9). The results of labour, as objects of consumption, have no fixity or permanence: food is produced not in order to endure but in order to be consumed (one does not 'use' food in the same sense as one 'uses' the table from which one eats it). Labour, then, reflects in its structure the reproductive cycle of the metabolic process. By contrast, *work* produces use-objects which are intended to last (the table rather than the food); in it, man as *homo faber* attains the status of artisan and creates the relatively permanent world of human artifacts, objects not of consumption but of utility. The structure of work is not, as with labour, cyclical but instrumental: the work-process 'is . . . entirely determined by the category of means and end' (*HC*, p. 143). *Action*, finally, creates no product but discloses the agent, realizes him, through his communication with other men. Because of its 'revelatory character' action entails the accompaniment of speech: the actor must be 'at the same time the speaker of words' and speechless action is a contradiction in terms (*HC*, pp. 178–9). Labour, work and action each involves a higher level of human self-realization and a higher level of consciousness: only in action does man take on his fully human stature.[10] Arendt sees man as worker finding his public sphere in 'the exchange market', although this is 'not . . . a political realm, properly speaking' (*HC*, p. 160). It is with action that the principle of the public sphere in the true (political) sense is established:

> Because of its inherent tendency to disclose the agent together with the act, action needs for its full appearance the shining brightness which we once called glory, and which is possible only within the public realm (*HC*, p. 180).

At the centre of Habermas's conceptual scheme is a system of three knowledge-constitutive human 'interests':

> The approach of the empirical-analytic sciences incorporates a *technical* cognitive interest; that of the historical-hermeneutic sciences incorporates a *practical* one; and the approach of critically oriented sciences incorporates the *emancipatory* cognitive interest . . .[11]

Habermas regards these interests as 'anthropologically' given, as having 'quasi-transcendental status' and as historically 'invariant'.[12] The crucial dividing line is that between the technical and the practical, between 'labour' and 'language' (*TP*, p. 9) or between *techne* and *praxis*.[13] On the technical side there is 'work' or 'purposive-rational action' and this is contrasted with 'interaction' or 'communicative action' (*TRS*, pp. 91–2). 'Work' is an affair of instrumental or goal-directed activity governed by technical rules, whereas 'interaction' has an entirely different structure, being an affair of communication involving a symbolic dimension (language) and governed by 'consensual norms'.[14] The aim of the emancipatory (critical) interest is the constitution of a society 'whose members' autonomy and responsibility had been realized' (*KHI*, p. 314) and in which there would exist 'uncoercive interaction on the basis of communication free from domination'.[15]

Critical theory thus directs itself against distorted communication whose roots are in 'the relations of power surreptitiously incorporated in the symbolic structures of the systems of speech and action' (*TP*, p. 12; cf. p. 22). One way in which relations of power distort communication and thereby stabilize the status quo is through the technification of the practical and of communicative action in general. The decline of the public sphere as a political institution is linked to the dominance of the technical (instrumental action) over the practical in modern society. The dominance of the technical leads to an increased 'scientization of politics', to a 'new politics, which is adapted to technical problems and brackets out practical questions' (*TRS*, pp. 106–7); and 'to the extent that practical questions are eliminated, the public realm loses its political function' (*TRS*, p. 104). In the same way, Arendt links the withering of the public realm with a 'reversal' in which action – in her meaning of the term – has become subordinated first to work and then to labour (*HC*, Ch. 6). The practical is displaced as purely technical – supposedly value-neutral – decisions supplant reflection on social norms and goals; science itself ceases to have the liberating function of enlightenment and becomes merely a productive force incorporated into the status quo.

Standing back from the conceptual schemes of Arendt and Habermas we can note first, the common concerns which underlie them.

Habermas's 'technical' relates to Arendt's 'labour' and 'work' together (though with a sharper focus on the latter); his 'practical' and more generally his dimension of 'interaction' relates to Arendt's 'action'. Behind both writers lies the influence of classical thought and especially of Aristotle's distinctions between productive and practical knowledge, between *techne* and *praxis*, between making (*poeisis*) and doing. For Aristotle it is politics which is the true – the authentically human – practice; '*praxis* is Aristotle's term for man's free activity in the realm of political·life'.[16] In this strict sense of the term productive activity is not *praxis* and the concept of *praxis* as essentially productive is alien to Aristotle's thought. Politics is for him the sphere of activity in which free men gain mutual recognition and thence self-realization through participation in the affairs of the *polis*: man is 'by nature a political animal'.[17] The conceptual schemes of Arendt and Habermas can be seen as affirming the continuing humanist relevance of this conception of the political – Arendt celebrates the *polis* as 'the space of men's free deeds and living words' (*OR*, p. 281) and Habermas invokes

Aristotle in his remark that 'The growth of the productive forces is not the same as the intention of the "good life". It can at best serve it' (*TRS*, p. 119).

The scheme developed by Habermas leads him into certain difficulties. For example, his attempted substitution of the concepts of work and interaction for Marx's concepts of the forces and relations of production (*TRS*, p. 113; *KHI*, p. 42) misses both the *broad* definition – including science, knowledge and the productive agents themselves – which Marx gives of the forces of production,[18] and also the way in which Marx by means of the concept of the relations of production seeks to grasp society as a totality structured through production as its dominant moment. Failing to see the 'totalizing' implications of Marx's concept of production, Habermas argues for a 'dialectic of moral life' (*KHI*, pp. 56 ff.) developing not through production but through cultural interaction and emancipatory struggle alone.

The thrust of Habermas's argument is against reductionism: he wants to establish the irreducible specificity of the different social 'moments'. The weakness of his view is that he carries his reaction against reductionism to the point where not the specificity of the moments but the overall unity of the totality becomes problematical. However, precisely because of the concern with the specific internal structure of each moment, the conceptual schemes of Habermas (work, interaction) and Arendt (labour, work, action) are of interest as they suggest ways of seeing the social totality as structured in terms of its various moments or dimensions.[19]

No doubt a further difficulty for Habermas concerns the status of his human 'interests' (see note 12, above). However, for the very reason that he regards them as 'anthropologically' grounded and historically 'invariant', Habermas can – unlike Marcuse – develop his characteristic themes without involving himself in a romantic protest against the technical as such. Whereas Marcuse envisages a utopian future in which, effectively, the technical is entirely dissolved into the practical, Habermas rejects the Marcusean view of nature as 'an opposing partner in a possible interaction' (*TRS*, p. 88). For him, the technical is an anthropologically given dimension of the human condition and therefore not something which can be abolished at some point in the future. In the same vein Marx emphasized that the production of use-values is 'the ever-lasting nature-imposed condition of human existence, and therefore is independent of every social phase of that existence, or, rather, is common to every such phase'; that there remains a realm of necessity (a realm of labour which must be undertaken as a means to ends external to it) 'in all social formations and under all possible modes of production'.[20]

The contrast on this issue between Habermas and Marcuse has its roots in an ambivalence characteristic of the Frankfurt School as a whole. Detailed discussion of it lies outwith the bounds of this paper.[21]

Conceptions of the political

For our purposes, the most crucial issue raised by the above accounts is the nature of the political as a dimension of social life.

In the past, Marxism has tended to see its conception of the political as secondary to its conception of the state: politics thus becomes an affair of asserting, or opposing the assertion of, state power. This approach leads to a view of revolutionary political practice as essentially goal-directed or instrumental ('technical' in Habermas's sense), as an affair of 'strategy' and 'tactics' alone. As a theoretical precondition of socialist democracy the irreducibility of the communicative, participatory or 'practical' dimension of revolutionary politics must be recognized alongside the instrumental. Moreover the 'practical' must be acknowledged not merely as something transitory, corresponding to a particular phase of revolutionary development, but as an essential moment of communist society itself.

Whereas instrumental politics, politics as the *techne* of power relations, can be regarded as perishing along with the state, the same cannot be said of participatory politics, politics as *praxis*. In Habermas's terms, communism can be described as *inter alia* an 'organization of society linked to decision-making on the basis of discussion free from domination' (*KHI*, p. 55). In this case, the practical-political not merely survives the death of the instrumental-political and the state but, under those new conditions, comes into its own and flourishes as never before.

These remarks imply a distinction between two senses of 'politics', a sense defined in terms of *power* relations and a sense defined in terms of *participation*.

We shall return to this distinction below. Although clearly it is rooted in many themes developed by the writers considered, their conceptual schemes do not draw it in quite the way the present argument requires.

Thus Arendt's reference to 'glory' in the passage where she establishes the connection between action and the public realm hints at a political romanticism and a conception of politics closer to Hobbes or Nietzsche than to Aristotle.[22] In Habermas, the 'practical' and the 'emancipatory' interests flow together: class struggle comes to be included under the general rubric of 'interaction' (*KHI*, pp. 42, 58–60). This elision of the two senses or aspects of 'politics' perhaps underlies his view that what makes a public sphere a political public sphere is that, in it, discussion deals with 'objects connected to the activity of the state'. This is to define politics in terms of the state as its 'object' and, taken literally, the passage suggests that the demise of the state signifies the demise of politics also.

In this connection it is interesting to refer to Wolin's view of politics as a mode of activity centring around 'the quest for competitive advantage'. This definition still sees the 'object' of politics in terms of competitive struggle but does not imply that this struggle involves the existence of *systematic* power relations such as underlie the state. The political would thus remain a dimension of society even without the state, for classless society would no doubt contain points of friction although these would no longer provide foci for the growth and extension of systematic relations of power.

Beyond both Habermas's and Wolin's conceptions of politics there remains, however, a third possibility: I shall indicate it in the broadest terms. Perhaps the specificity of the practical-political may be seen as lying not in its concern with the state or with competitive struggle but in its 'general' (Wolin) or 'universal' nature. Like Rousseau's general will, truly political debate 'should spring from all and apply to all'[23] and this may be its defining feature. Of course, debate could deal with matters of 'universal' concern and yet consist of different groups 'competitively' pressing their own particular interests. A more rigorous model is implied in Rousseau's view that in public debate what is asked of a people 'is not precisely whether they approve of the proposition or reject it, but whether it is in conformity with the general will which is theirs'.[24] This universalistic approach may afford a conception of the nature of political *praxis*, engaged and yet personally disinterested, in communist society.

A final preliminary question remains: granted that the political endures as a specific *dimension or moment* of social existence, does it endure also as a specific *area* (a 'sphere' or 'realm') of social life? It might be argued that the concept of a political public sphere becomes redundant in communist society not because the political has withered away but because society has become political throughout, in its every pore. No fundamental argument of the present paper turns on the answer to this question and so I shall merely express a personal opinion. As a sphere of 'universal' debate the political has an essentially unitary character. Even granted the conditions obtaining in communist society, it seems utopian to expect that the political can be diffused throughout society without its unitary and hence its universal nature being lost in the sands of particularistic local or group perspectives. For this reason, in what follows, I shall speak not merely of the political but of a political public sphere in connection with communist society.

Communism and the public sphere

I shall argue for two theses: (i) that a true (universal and undistorted) public sphere presupposes communism; and (ii) that communism in turn involves the existence of a practical-political dimension, a political public sphere. The present section is concerned with thesis (i).

Why does the existence of a true political public sphere presuppose communism? Habermas himself gives a large part of the answer when, in the course of his definition, he says: 'Access [to the public sphere] is guaranteed to all citizens.' The bourgeois public sphere was accessible only to the middle classes and when, in the nineteenth century, 'the public body expanded beyond the bourgeoisie' (i.e. when it began to include the proletariat) the minimum of coherence and consensus necessary for meaningful public discussion broke down and the public sphere became 'a field for the competition of interests'.[25]

There seem to be two alternatives in a class-divided society: either (a) access to the public sphere is granted to only *one* class or (b) the communication on which public discussion is premised is distorted by what we have seen Habermas describe as 'the relations of power surreptitiously incorporated in the symbolic structures of the systems of speech and action' (*TP*, p. 12; see also p. 22). If alternative (a) is followed then the 'public' character of the public sphere – its openness to *all* citizens for the discussion of genuinely public ('universal') concerns – is compromised. (Of course, the circle can be squared by recognizing as 'citizens' only a restricted class or classes: this was the solution of Ancient democracy.) If alternative (b) is followed then the public sphere decays as in fact it has done in the advanced capitalist societies.

In short, the existence of a true political public sphere presupposes community of interests and where – as in class-divided societies – this community is absent then it can exist only in an impure, restricted or distorted, form. (On the other hand, to say that it exists only in impure and distorted form is by no means to say that it does not exist at all.)

On this issue we can learn a good deal by turning once again to the political theory of Rousseau. The central question for Rousseau's theory is: under what conditions can the general will (the will of the community *qua* community) be clearly known and expressed?

One still-influential interpretation replies that Rousseau's concept of the general will is totalitarian, inducive of artificially engineered unanimity and involving the total suppression of anything resembling a public sphere.[26] However, a quite different account may be offered, viz., that on the contrary the general will can be known and gain a clear expression only given the existence of a public sphere open to all citizens. It is true that Rousseau does maintain that the general will gains clearest expression in the absence of 'sectional associations' (*des associations partielles*) but he adds at once that 'if there are sectional associations [i.e. if ideal conditions do not obtain], it is wise to multiply their number and to prevent inequality among them'.[27] In the same way, he holds that unanimity can be a sign not of a clear expression of the general will but of its very opposite.[28] In short, for Rousseau knowledge of the general will can emerge only through full and free discussion, through participation in legislation: politics in the 'practical' sense is the very foundation of his imagined state.

Two requirements are imposed by Rousseau on his utopia: that it be small and that it have no (class) divisions of economic interest. The first of these harks back to the face-to-face communication of the classical *polis* and is evidently unrealistic. The second emerges when Rousseau says that the general will, unlike the will of all, 'studies only the common interest'; and when he says that it 'derives its generality less from the number of voices than from the common interest which unites them'.[29] That Rousseau understands this common interest in socio-economic terms is clear from passages such as the following:

> Do you want coherence in a state? Then bring the two extremes as close together as possible; have neither very rich men nor beggars, for these two estates, naturally inseparable, are equally fatal to the common good.

. . . no citizen shall be rich enough to buy another and none so poor as to be forced to sell himself.[30]

Thus Rousseau sees very clearly that the existence of a public sphere and undistorted communication (the integrity of the 'practical' or, in his terms, the clear articulation of the general will) presupposes community of interest and absence of class divisions. (It is indeed in this utopian context that his hostility towards sectional associations should be understood. His second-best recommendation regarding the multiplicity of associations says, in effect, that where a truly universalistic political *praxis* is impossible at any rate the extension of systematic power relations should be avoided. Given the *de facto* existence of systematic power relations this is to a large extent unrealistic.) Of course, it is true that Rousseau envisages the community of interests whose necessity he recognizes in essentially petty-bourgeois terms: everyone should have sufficient and none too much.[31] However, we can learn from him that only on a foundation of common interest can politics in the participatory sense, communicative action in a public sphere, be present in undistorted form. What Rousseau holds to be realizable in a petty-bourgeois utopia the Marxist can apply *mutatis mutandis* to fully developed communism.

The introduction of Rousseau at this point in our discussion is not accidental: Colletti develops the interesting argument that Rousseau anticipates the Marxist thesis of the withering away of the state.[32] I shall return below to the question of the state under communism; already it can be seen that the disappearance of class antagonisms (and thus of the state) is arguably a precondition for political practice in Rousseau himself. The death of the state is, I suggest, a necessary premise for a true political public sphere.

Revolution and the public sphere

So far, it has been argued that a political public sphere ideally presupposes a degree of undistorted communication which in turn presupposes a community of interests that, for a Marxist, is realized only with communism. Class power relations produce structures of distorted communication and the public realm is flawed.

I do not wish to argue, however, that a public sphere is a remote end of political action which must be sought with quite different (e.g. purely instrumental as opposed to practical, or with outrightly repressive) means. The constitution of a universal and undistorted public realm is not a distant goal of revolutionary action but, rather, a progressively realized moment at all stages of on-going struggle: revolutionary politics, as already commented, must be practical and participatory as well as instrumental. The revolutionary process must be democratic at every step as new classes and new areas of social and personal life are brought into a previously restricted public realm. The struggle against distorted structures of communication is an ever-present revolutionary concern and by no means something which can be postponed to the future.

In terms of socialist democracy the constitution of a sphere of unconstrained communication is an end in itself. However, it is also a necessary condition in the most 'technical' sense for revolution in advanced capitalist society: the power of the bourgeoisie cannot be broken without a continual struggle for the enlargement and restructuring of the public sphere. This emerges most clearly from Gramsci's views on the importance of hegemonic control ('direction' as distinct from 'domination' or coercion) in the West as compared to the more backward state structures confronted by the Bolsheviks:

> In Russia the state was everything, civil society was primordial and gelatinous; in the West, there was a proper relation between state and civil society, and when the state trembled a sturdy structure of civil society was at once revealed. The state was only an outer ditch, behind which there stood a powerful system of fortresses and earthworks. . . .[33]

The increased importance of ideological hegemony for social control implies that it is *inter alia* through the distortion of the public sphere that the position of the bourgeoisie is maintained. Struggle for the restructuring of the public sphere as a means of countering bourgeois hegemony takes on a crucial significance under advanced capitalism: revolution in such societies literally cannot be accomplished if the old structures of distorted communication remain intact.

What has been said on the revolutionary constitution of the public sphere raises important questions regarding the institutional forms of the transition to socialism and thence to communism: in no way must these forms relegate the 'practical' dimension of revolutionary politics to a secondary or inessential position.

The crucial question is that of the Leninist model of the revolutionary political party. For Lenin, the party is necessary because 'the working class, exclusively by its own efforts, is able to develop only trade union consciousness'; 'Class political consciousness can be brought to the workers *only from without'*.[34] Arendt argues that such a view entails the very negation of a public realm: 'Wherever knowing and doing have parted company, the space of freedom is lost' (*OR*, p. 264). She turns from the party to 'the council system, the always defeated but only authentic outgrowth of every revolution since the eighteenth century',[35] and with great eloquence celebrates the 'councils, *soviets* and *Räte*", the 'townships and town-hall meetings' of revolutionary America and the 'revolutionary societies and municipal councils' of the early days of revolutionary France. If the aim of revolution is 'freedom and the constitution of a public space where freedom could appear'[36] then only the council system can, in her view, ensure the opportunity for participation in public affairs with which that freedom is bound up. Echoing Rosa Luxemburg, Arendt praises that 'spontaneity' against which Lenin directs his most powerful arguments (*OR*, Ch. 6; cf. *HC*, p. 216 note).

These issues can only very briefly be discussed here. Lenin's emphasis on the party did not prevent him from seeing 'the dictatorship of the proletariat' in terms of popular involvement in organization and decision-making – a massive opening of the public sphere to previously excluded classes. He stresses the need to develop 'in creative organizational work' the 'independent initiative' of the working and exploited people, and also the need to break with the prejudice 'that only the so-called "upper classes", only the rich, and those who have gone through the school of the rich, are capable of administering the state and directing the organizational development of socialist society'.[37]

Moreover, if an important aim of revolution is to constitute a 'universal' public realm, political society 'in its general sense', then it may be that a council structure encourages too localized, too inward-looking an approach to public affairs. Arendt felt the need to demarcate councils on her model from 'the communes of hippies and drop-outs' which she saw (rightly) as stemming from 'a renunciation of the whole of public life, of politics in general'.[38] It may be that such an anti-political (i.e. anti-'universal', anti-'public') tendency lies at the basis of the council system generally, notwithstanding the élan of the 'heroic' days of revolution itself. A localized debate-structure can lead to evasion of some of the most difficult *global* problems revolutionary society must face and it is perhaps here that the party finds its indispensable political, 'practical' role.

Objections to Marx

In the light of their conceptual schema outlined above, Arendt and Habermas press a line of objection to Marx which raises extremely important issues. Consideration of their objections will lead us to substantiation of the second thesis given earlier: that not merely does a true public sphere entail communism but communism in turn must evolve the practical-political dimension present in a public sphere.

In sum, Marx is accused of *reducing* the 'practical' dimension of communicative interaction and critical struggle to the 'technical' dimension of labour or work. He is accused of allowing no space to the political, in the practical sense of a public sphere. It would follow from these charges that the notion of a Marxist political theory – such as the present paper seeks to develop – would be simply a contradiction in terms, and that attempts to give the concept of socialist democracy a rigorous Marxist grounding must remain quixotic.

Thus Arendt sees Marx as a philosopher of (in her sense) 'labour': his view in *The German Ideology* of men distinguishing themselves from animals when they begin to produce their means of subsistence she regards as 'the very content of the definition of man as *animal laborans*' (*HC*, p. 99, note 36) – i.e. of man as sunk in the metabolic cycle of life.

Further, she finds in the Marxist idea of the withering away of the state evidence that Marx is complicit in that erosion of the public realm which, as we have seen, is her main concern (*HC*, pp. 44–5, 60). Habermas's charge is similar. 'At the level of his material investigations . . . Marx always takes account of social practice that encompasses both work and interaction'; however the interactive, emancipatory aspect of practice 'is not made part of the philosophical frame of reference' (*KHI*, pp. 53, 42). Marx, he argues, did indeed sense the dialectic of labour and interaction (*KHI*, p. 55; *TP*, p. 168); however

> Marx does not actually explicate the interrelationship of interaction and labour, but instead, under the unspecific title of social praxis, reduces the one to the other, namely: communicative action to instrumental action. . . .
> . . . for Marx instrumental action, the productive activity which regulates the material interchange of the human species with its natural environment, becomes the paradigm for the generation of all the categories; everything is resolved into the self-movement of production (*TP*, pp. 168–9).

Marx, that is, reduces communicative interaction to work. Indeed, the emancipatory or critical as well as the practical interest is subsumed under the technical so that there is a two-fold, interconnected result: the moment of interaction essential to the public sphere is defined out and the way is paved for the reduction of Marxism from 'critique' to 'positive science' (*KHI*, pp. 44–6, 62–3; *TP*, pp. 169, 238–9).

Habermas further argues that Marx's alleged reductionism vitiates his conception of communist society: Marx's vision is premised upon belief in 'the optimistic convergence of technology and democracy'; 'Marx equates the practical insight of a political public with successful technical control' (*TRS*, pp. 60, 58; cf. *TP*, p. 169). This is the objection which Adorno sums up in his reported comment that Marx wanted to turn the world into a 'giant workhouse'.[39]

But did Marx really believe that a society organized in terms of maximum technical rationality would also be, automatically and by that very token, an optimally free society? Did he, in effect, define political freedom in terms of technical efficiency?

Two fundamental questions are raised by Arendt's and Habermas's objections. Does Marx exclude any 'practical-political' moment, any dimension of communicative action or *praxis* in the Aristotle-Habermas sense from his concept of *production*? And: does he exclude and 'practical-political' moment from his conception of *communism*? Clearly these questions are related but it will be convenient to consider each in turn.

Marx's concept of production

Under this head we may consider first Arendt's charge that Marx reduces 'action' and 'work' to 'labour'.

Her characterization of Marx as a philosopher of 'labour' seems perverse although, as we shall see, the apparent perversity has its roots in an important misunderstanding. For whatever may be said about 'action', it is certainly the case that 'work' receives a sharp focus in Marx's writings. (Indeed, the degeneration of 'work' into 'labour', diagnosed by Arendt, is for Marx a symptom of alienation.) Thus in 1844 Marx stresses that unlike animals 'man produces even when he is free from physical need and only truly produces himself in freedom therefrom . . . An animal's product belongs immediately to its physical body, whilst man freely confronts his product.'[40] *Pace* Arendt, and adapting her own words, this is surely the very content of the definition of man as *homo faber*, as artisan or worker. Truly human production does not merely serve the physical reproductive metabolism, but man 'freely confronts' his product, that is, confronts it as something lasting and independent. Distinctively human products are artifacts, not mere phases in the cycle of consumption. The characteristic structure of 'work' (as opposed to 'labour') emerges too in another passage, one that is pivotal for the dialectic of *Capital*:

> We presuppose labour in a form that stamps it as exclusively human. A spider conducts operations that resemble those of a weaver, and a bee puts to shame many an architect in the construction of her cells. But what distinguishes the worst architect from the best of bees is this, that the architect raises his structure in imagination before he erects it in reality. At the end of every labour-process, we get a result that already existed in the imagination of the labourer at its commencement.[41]

Here, Marx focuses on precisely the instrumental means-end structure which Arendt takes to be characteristic of 'work'. She knows this passage and indeed quotes it, adding: 'Obviously, Marx [here] no longer speaks of labour, but of work – with which he is not concerned . . .' (*HC*, p. 99, note; cf. p. 87). Need more be said? Marx does not reduce work to labour, though shortly we shall see what leads Arendt to argue in this way.

But does Marx reduce 'action' to 'work'/'labour'? In Habermas's terms: does his conception of production involve a reduction of communicative to instrumental action, of the practical and the critical to the technical?

On the face of it this seems unlikely. Marx saw production as essentially social or communal in character and thus as involving a moment of practical interaction, of *praxis*. This is clear from the following:

> The human being is in the most literal sense a *zoon politikon*, not merely a gregarious animal, but an animal which can individuate itself only in the midst of society. Production by an isolated individual outside society . . . is as much an absurdity as is the development of language without individuals living *together* and talking to each other.[42]

To be sure, Marx here as elsewhere speaks of man as social rather than as specifically political – but the impressive point is the comparison with language. As we have seen, language and communication (Habermas) and speech (Arendt) are of the very essence of the practical-political, of *praxis*. Moreover Marx includes 'general social knowledge', surely a 'communicative' element, among the forces of production.[43] If 'exclusively human' production is 'conscious' production, then arguably that consciousness is communicative or 'political' consciousness. I would suggest that Marx regards the practical-political dimension as intrinsic to the concept of production itself; that, in other words, production (i.e. specifically human production) involves for him a practical-political moment.

This impression is strengthened if we consider what, according to Marx, are the products of economic production. These are two-fold: use-values and the social relations (structured as relations of production).[44] And since 'the human essence' is 'the ensemble of the social relations'[45] it follows that, in producing his social relations, man is at the same time producing himself. Marx regards man as, through the mediation of his social relations, a self-producer. This is indeed why Arendt sees him as a philosopher of 'labour': in the spirit of Feuerbach's 'Man is what he eats' Marx sometimes expresses man's self-production in 'physiological' terms and the *German Ideology* passage cited by Arendt is one such instance. What she fails to see is that the notion of self-production does not reduce Marx's view of *praxis* to 'labour' but, rather, establishes as an irreducible moment within it 'action', practice, *praxis* in the Aristotelian 'political' sense discussed above. For men produce themselves not merely as results of the production process but in and through participation in the production process itself. Men produce themselves in 'how' rather than in 'what' they produce, in the *form* of their products (or, rather, in 'what' only insofar as 'what' is a determinant of 'how'). Their products are a unity of content (use-value, 'what') and form (social relations defining human essence, 'how'). Thus Marx can write:

> This mode of production must not be considered simply as being the production of the physical existence of these individuals. Rather it is a definite form of expressing their life, a definite *mode of life* on their part. As individuals express their life, so they are. What they are, therefore, coincides with their production, both with *what* they produce and *how* they produce.[46]

In this passage, the what/how distinction invokes the distinction Aristotle draws between production and practice and between making and doing: 'while "making" aims at an end different from the very act of "making", the end of "doing" is nothing else but the act of "doing" itself performed well'.[47] In terms of this distinction it is difficult to resist the conclusion that Marx's concept of production involves both production in the restricted sense *and* communicative practice. If production is seen as the self-production of man then its *practical* dimension ('how' rather than 'what') takes on a new importance. Marx's fusion of production with practice and interaction is by no means a reduction of the latter to the former but, rather, the formulation of a new – essentially un-Aristotelian – concept: that of *productive practice* or *practical production.*

The structure of production is thus not exhausted by the notion of instrumental action as exemplified in the passage from *Capital* cited above. Rather, Marx is concerned to develop a structured concept of productive practice as a totality in which both moments, the technical and the practical (together with the emancipatory), work and communicative interaction, economics and (critical, participatory) politics, are in their specificity preserved.

It was remarked above that Habermas's reaction against 'reductionism' leads him to a point where the overall unity of the social totality is called in question. Marxism, by contrast, is concerned with 'explaining the connection and *complexus* [of social life] precisely in so far as it is a connection and a *complexus*'.[48]

A long footnote in *Knowledge and Human Interests* (note 14 to Ch. 3: pp. 326–9) shows that Habermas entirely misses the point of Marx's attempt in his 1857 Introduction to develop the notion of a totality with production as its dominant moment. However, an important question is raised for Marxism: how should the concept of a totality structured through production be related to the structural specificity of the totality's different moments or dimensions? I would suggest that the notion of a non-reductionist totality must be grounded in the concept of human self-production, at once practical or interactive and (in the narrow sense of the term) productive. Further discussion is impossible here, but I would add only that, in the light of my suggestion, Habermas's attempt to give an 'anthropological' grounding to the dimensions of social life is perhaps not without foundation.[49]

Passing on from Habermas's more particular criticisms, it may be useful to set Marx's concept of production in the context of similar themes in Hegel. As has been noted, for Aristotle it is politics which is the truly human *praxis.* In his dialectic of Master and Slave, Hegel 'inverts' Aristotle and, with enormous consequences for modern thought as a whole, identifies as the true *praxis* not the politics of the

Master but the productive labour (economics) of the Slave.[50] The Master is recognized in his humanity by the Slave and is seemingly the 'essential' self-consciousness; but since the Slave is not recognized by the Master this recognition counts for nothing. Moreover the Master is dependent on the productive labour of the Slave. 'The truth of the independent consciousness is accordingly the consciousness of the bondsman.'[51] It is the labour of the Slave which goes on to create a human world; in Kojève's phrase, the Master is in an 'existential impasse'.

Hegel, Marx tells us, 'grasps labour as the essence of man',[52] and nowhere is this more true than in the dialectic of Master and Slave. It may be asked whether this conception of labour (which for Hegel is ultimately and 'in the last instance' the labour of Spirit) is reductionist; whether Hegel, and Marx too by association, reduces practice to instrumental labour *simpliciter*.

I have suggested that Marx for his part is not reductionist but wishes by means of the concept of *praxis* to comprehend a totality of human self-production, a totality including as its moments not only production of use-values but communicative interaction (politics, practice, *praxis* in Aristotle's sense) as well. As regards Hegel the position is less clear.[53] The final stage or goal of the Hegelian dialectic is not the world of human and social institutions (Ethical Life, the culmination of Objective Spirit) but philosophy (the culmination of Absolute Spirit). There is a parallel here in Aristotle's account of contemplation.[54] For Hegel, philosophy is a monologue of a total, unitary self-consciousness: Absolute Spirit stands alone. The plurality of selves presupposed by a practical public sphere is dissolved into the unity of the Absolute.

It is of the greatest interest that Feuerbach, in his critique of Hegel, insists on just the dimension of communicative interaction which Hegel's monistic conception of philosophy denies:

> The true dialectic is not a monologue of a solitary thinker with himself; it is a dialogue between I and Thou.[55]

Moreover, it is precisely the fact that he 'makes the social relationship "of man to man" the basic principle of his theory' that Marx in 1844 finds admirable in Feuerbach's treatment of Hegel.[56] However, Hegel himself by no means excludes unambiguously the moment of communicative action and in one eloquent passage recognizes it as fundamental:

For the nature of humanity is to struggle for agreement with others, and its very existence lies simply in the explicit realization of a community of conscious life.[57]

This 'community of conscious life' is, surely, the sphere of communicative interaction on which Habermas *et al.* insist.

We can now pose our second question: is Marx's communism a 'community of conscious life' in this sense or is it a substitution of technical (instrumental) rationality for communicative action? Does communism in Marx's conception involve the dimension which in its specificity constitutes a public sphere?

Marx's concept of communism

A positive answer to this question is suggested by the preceding discussion: if Marx's concept of production and self-production involves a practical moment, then it is hardly likely that his view of communist society, where truly human production will for the first time flourish, would simply ignore this moment and reduce communism to technocracy.

This positive answer receives further confirmation from Marx's definition of communism as 'the real appropriation of the human essence by and for man',[58] because consciousness is for him a dimension intrinsic to specifically human existence and, further, consciousness is necessarily linked with language:

> Language is as old as consciousness, language *is* practical consciousness that exists also for other men, and for that reason alone it really exists for me personally as well; language, like consciousness, only arises from the need, the necessity, of intercourse with other men.[59]

'Language is the immediate actuality of thought',[60] says Marx, influenced no doubt by the passage from Feuerbach just cited and also by Hegel's statement that 'language is self-consciousness existing for others'.[61] This (extremely 'modern') insistence on language as intrinsic to consciousness which in its turn is intrinsic to man's essence (to be realized under communism) shows that Marx's conception of communism does not *prima facie* exclude the moment of communicative interaction, of politics or *praxis*.

However, as we have seen, it is the concept of the withering away of the state which has seemed to commentators such as Arendt to commit

Marxism to a conception of communism in which the political public realm is eroded and suffocated by 'society'. Apparently supporting such an interpretation is Engels's statement, explicitly derived from Saint-Simon, that with the withering away of the state 'the government of persons is replaced by the administration of things'.[62] The virtues of this formulation apart, it is however difficult to see why the withering away of the state should entail the withering away of the 'political' in the sense so far discussed. Certainly there is a sense of the 'political' in which the demise of the state (premised on class divisions and alienation) involves an end of politics: Marx says, for example, that with the advent of communism 'social evolutions will cease to be political revolutions' and that 'public power will lose its political character'.[63]

Clearly, two senses of 'politics' must be distinguished: the sense in which politics will wither away with the demise of the state and the sense in which politics will endure (and, I would argue, come into its own for the first time in history).

Earlier, we introduced a distinction between 'instrumental' and 'practical' politics, between politics as defined in terms of power and politics as defined in terms of the *praxis* of participation in a public sphere. Of these two aspects or dimensions it is the 'power' aspect which has so far received the sharpest focus in the Marxist tradition. Marx writes that 'political power . . . is merely the organized power of one class for oppressing the other'[64] and Lenin also concentrates on this aspect in his theory of the state. This emphasis is of course not accidental: in class society the power aspect of politics dominates the practical with (at best) distorted structures of communication and (at worst) outright repression as the typical results. However, a close concentration on politics as the *techne* of class power relations has had the unfortunate 'side-effect' of drawing attention away from a 'practical' conception of politics which could provide a theoretical support for socialist democracy and which could help clarify the nature of freedom and participation under communism.

In communist society, in the absence of class divisions and alienation, the state withers away[65] and with it the instrumental-political, the politics of power. Conversely, politics in the sense of participation, political *praxis*, will – precisely because the stranglehold of class power-relations is broken – flourish as never before.

The crucial distinction is, then, between politics as *participation* (*praxis*) and politics as *power*.[66]

In the history of political theory it can be said, broadly, that the two political dimensions correspond to the 'classical' and the 'modern' conceptions of politics. The conception of politics as participation is implicit in Aristotle (though hardly at all in Plato),[67] while the 'power' conception is developed most dramatically at the dawn of the bourgeois era by Machiavelli and Hobbes. In an important essay, Habermas formulates the change as one from political theory as 'the doctrine of the good and just life; . . . the continuation of ethics' to political theory as (in Machiavelli) 'the art . . . of permanent strategies for asserting one's power' (*TP*, Ch. 1, pp. 42, 50). The participatory and power conceptions each entail a different notion of political 'recognition': in the classical view recognition is gained through mutual interaction (in the *polis*) while in the modern view recognition is sought through power itself in a dialectic whose crucial terms are 'pride' and 'fear'.[68]

At a theoretical level, the two conceptions of politics are complementary while at the historical level they are polar opposites. Under capitalism the power dimension distorts – albeit 'surreptitiously' – the public sphere, while under communism the participatory dimension, politics as *praxis*, grows and develops in the absence of distorting power relations.

Thus with communism the classical definition of man as a political being comes into its own: just as the practical-political itself comes into its own in the truly 'universal' sense indicated above. The real 'history' of mankind, to adopt Marx's usage in the 1859 Preface, develops not through a dialectic of power conflicts but by way of dialogue through the involvement of the mass of the people in that 'analysis of the quality, direction and fate of public life' (Wolin) which is the essence of the public sphere.

Communism is an 'organization of society linked to decision-making on the basis of discussion free from domination' (Habermas) and initiates what Walter Benjamin aptly describes as 'the literarization of all relationships of life'.[69] Indeed, a communist public sphere would draw into itself the widest possible range of topics and interests: production decisions which today are taken on purely 'technical' grounds (thereby furthering capitalist interests) as well as much which today still seems of 'private' concern (sex, friendship, the family). As a 'space of men's free deeds and living words' (Arendt) a communist public sphere would bring to men's actions and their lives as a whole that clarity and enlightenment which have been the dream of the radical tradition for two hundred years.

Conclusion

I have argued that the concept of a true political public sphere presupposes communist society and that it is an authentic and irreducible moment of such a society. The distinction between the two dimensions of politics, the power dimension and the practical-political, makes it possible to argue that the latter by no means perishes along with the state.

As we have seen, the shadow of 'power' clings to both Arendt's and Habermas's definitions of the political and on these premises the death of the state must indeed mean the death of politics as such. However, if the definition of the practical-political indicated above – in terms of its universal constituency and concerns – is accepted, then for us this is no longer the case. Not only does the concept of a true public sphere entail communism: communism entails and indeed liberates from the restricting and distorting pressure of power relations a true political public sphere.

Here we may return to Marx's distinction between the realms of necessity and of freedom, a distinction which finds its echo in Habermas's contrast of the technical and the practical. For Marx the realm of freedom is the site of 'that development of human energy which is an end in itself',[70] that is, the sphere of the practical and the interactive, of self-development through participation and debate. I have argued that this practical-political moment is intrinsic not only to Marx's conception of communism but to his conception of production itself.

It would, however, be inappropriate to end with a 'long' view of the flourishing of the practical under full communism: half a century of history leaves a darker impression. Stalin's destruction of the socialist public sphere was the precondition of a repression so extensive that 'not one of the tyrants and despots of the past persecuted and destroyed so many of his compatriots'.[71] If, as Wolin and others suggest, the vocation of political theory is the defence and constitution of the political, then Marxism cannot afford not to see itself within the context of the tradition of political theory. A lively sense of the political is a necessary condition of socialist democracy and – in the advanced capitalist societies – of revolution itself. The concept of the political as *praxis* provides theoretical grounding for the thesis that revolutionary transition must and can only be democratic. Marxism as a matter of urgency must develop a political theory.

NOTES

1. Wolin, *Politics and Vision* (Little, Brown), pp. 288, 432.
2. Ibid., pp. 10–11.
3. Habermas, *Toward a Rational Society* (Heinemann) [hereafter: *TRS*], p. 75.
4. Habermas, 'The Public Sphere: An Encyclopedia Article (1964)', *New German Critique*, Vol. 1, No. 3 (Fall 1974).
5. Arendt, *On Revolution* (Penguin), pp. 33, 103; *The Human Condition* (University of Chicago Press), pp. 199, 220. Hereafter, these works will be referenced as (respectively) *OR* and *HC*.
6. In the political sphere, says Arendt, 'speech rules supreme' (*OR*, p. 35; see also *HC*, Ch. 5 passim). Cf. *OR*, p. 19: 'The two famous definitions of man by Aristotle, that he is a political being and a being endowed with speech, supplement each other and both refer to the same experience in Greek *polis* life.'
7. *HC*, pp. 220, 41; cf. Wolin, op. cit., pp. 287, 290.
8. Wolin, 'Political Theory as a Vocation' in Martin Fleisher, ed., *Machiavelli and the Nature of Political Thought* (Croom Helm), p. 26.
9. See Lucio Colletti's criticism of Marcuse in his *From Rousseau to Lenin* (NLB), pp. 137–40.
10. See further Noel O'Sullivan on Arendt in A. de Crespigny and K. Minogue, eds., *Contemporary Political Philosophers* (Methuen), pp. 229 ff.
11. Habermas, *Knowledge and Human Interests* (Heinemann) [hereafter: *KHI*], p. 308; cf. p. 313: 'knowledge-constitutive interests take form in the medium of work, language and power'. See also Habermas, *Theory and Practice* (Heinemann) [hereafter: *TP*], pp. 7–10. Habermas's tripartite division corresponds to Aristotle's division of knowledge into three types: theoretical, practical and productive – with the difference that, in Habermas, critical theory is substituted for theory on the traditional model.
12. *TP*, p. 8; for some of the problems to which this approach gives rise, see pp. 14–15. Recognition of these interests is said to characterize critical as distinct from traditional or positivist theory (*KHI*, p. 308; *TP*, p. 9). By grounding critical theory in a concept of human interests, Habermas seeks to free it from the historicist relativism which had characterized earlier Frankfurt positions: see *TRS*, p. 113.
13. Interestingly, Habermas says that it was in part Arendt who 'called my attention to the fundamental significance of the Aristotelian distinction between *techne* and *praxis*' (*TP*, p. 286, note 4 to Ch. 1).
14. A similar distinction is developed by John Rawls, 'Two Concepts of Rules', in Philippa Foot, ed., *Theories of Ethics* (Oxford).
15. *KHI*, p. 58; see also pp. 53, 55, 310, 315.
16. N. Lobkowicz, *Theory and Practice: History of a Concept from Aristotle to Marx* (Notre Dame), p. 11.
17. See Aristotle, *Politics*, Bk. I (Penguin edn., p. 28).
18. See Marx, *The Poverty of Philosophy* (International Publishers), p. 174; *Grundrisse* (Penguin Books), pp. 422, 540, 706, 711; *Capital*, Vol. I (Allen & Unwin), p. 355. Cf. Georg Lukács's critique of Bukharin in his *Political Writings 1919–1929* (NLB), pp. 136 ff.
19. For passages in Marx's writings which imply a view of society not as divided into

base and superstructure (as in the 1859 Preface) but as a Unitary totality, see *Poverty of Philosophy*, pp. 110–11, and *Grundrisse*, pp. 99–100, 278. An important question for Marxists is how this totality is organized or structured. Concerned to avoid reductionism, Louis Althusser sees the social totality as a structure of discrete 'practices' or 'instances'; however, he regards each of these practices as having the same, homologous internal structure of production – see *For Marx* (Allen Lane), pp. 166 ff. He is thus driven back on a merely abstract insistence on plurality and in the end his position (like that of Engels in his letters of the 1890s remains merely ambiguous as between economic reductionism and pluralism. By contrast the various 'practices' given by Arendt and Habermas are distinguished precisely in terms of their internal specific structures: e.g. work is goal-directed whereas interaction is not. Such schema suggest the possibility of a typology of non-homologous practices, each defined in terms of its specific structure, which 'cohere' in virtue of their concrete interrelations into a (non-reductionist) totality. A problem, however, remains: a programme of this sort would have to relate itself to the Marxian view of the social totality as structured (totalized) through its dominant moment, viz., economic production. Discussion of this problem cannot be undertaken here.

20. *Capital* (Lawrence & Wishart), Vol. I, pp. 163–4; Vol. III, p. 820. In *The German Ideology* (Lawrence & Wishart complete edition, 1965), pp. 87, 96 and p. 45 on the division of labour and the *Critique of the Gotha Programme* (Moscow, p. 18), Marx seems to believe that the 'technical', the 'realm of necessity', can indeed be abolished. This attitude has its roots in the 1844 *Manuscripts* (Lawrence & Wishart, p. 69) where he holds that labour is alienated when it is not an end in itself but 'merely a means to satisfy needs external to it'. In 1844 Marx sees communism as the resolution of the conflict 'between man and nature', as well as 'between man and man' (op. cit., p. 95). However, in the *Grundrisse* (Penguin: esp. p. 712 – 'Labour cannot become play, as Fourier would like') and *Capital* (loc. cit.) he takes the more realistic view that with communism only the conflict between man and man can be abolished, and not that between man and nature. (Moreover, I consider that the thesis of a dialectics of nature is an attempt – by means of a romantic conception of nature dressed in the garb of science – to sustain the belief that the conflict between man and nature can be overcome.)

21. The *locus* of this ambivalence is Horkheimer and Adorno's *Dialectic of Enlightenment* (Allen Lane) which affirms both that Enlightenment 'already contains the seed' of totalitarianism and administered life and that 'social freedom is inseparable from enlightened thought' (p. xiii). The work marks a turning-point in the development of the Frankfurt School: the earlier orientation (e.g. Marcuse's *Reason and Revolution*) was premised on a 'popular front' linking critical theory and Enlightenment rationalism; but once the structure of Enlightenment thought itself seemed a structure of domination ('. . . for the rulers, men become material, just as nature as a whole is material for society'; 'Mastery over nature is reproduced within humanity': Horkheimer and Adorno, op. cit., pp. 87, 110), the way out could lie only in a romantic *Aufhebung* of the purposive-rational structure of Enlightenment thought itself. This is the problematic of Marcuse's *One-Dimensional Man* (see the passages cited by Habermas in *TRS*, p. 86); it reaches its apogee in the romantic cult of the 'New Sensibility' in his *An Essay on Liberation*. An excellent discussion of these issues is to be found in Alfred Schmidt's *The Concept of Nature in Marx* (NBL) passim.

22. Cf. O'Sullivan, op. cit., pp. 231–2. However, as O'Sullivan points out, Arendt also distances herself from such a conception in a revealing comment on Hobbes and Nietzsche: see *HC*, p. 203.

23. Rousseau, *The Social Contract*, Bk. II, Ch. 4.

24. Ibid., Bk IV, Ch. 2.

25. 'The Public Sphere . . .', op. cit.

26. See, e.g. J. L. Talmon, *The Origins of Totalitarian Democracy* (Sphere), Part 1.

27. *Social Contract*, Bk II, Ch. 3.

28. 'This is when the citizens, lapsed into servitude, have no longer either freedom or will. Then fear of flattery turns voting into acclamation; people no longer deliberate, they worship or curse' (op. cit., Bk IV, Ch. 2).

29. Ibid., Bk. II, Ch. 3 and Bk. II, Ch. 4.

30. Ibid., Bk. II, Ch. 11.

31. See Lucien Goldmann, *The Philosophy of the Enlightenment* (Routledge and Kegan Paul), p. 38: 'Rousseau's ideal seems to be a kind of petit-bourgeois democracy, whose members are both free and equal, and none very rich or very poor.'

32. *From Rousseau to Lenin*, pp. 180–7.

33. Gramsci, *Selections from the Prison Notebooks* (Lawrence & Wishart), p. 238; for accounts of Gramsci's concept of hegemony see Carl Boggs, *Gramsci's Marxism* (Pluto Press), Ch. 2, and Gwyn A. Williams, 'The Concept of 'Egemonia' in the Thought of Gramsci: Some Notes on Interpretation', *Journal of the History of Ideas*, Vol. 21 (1960).

34. Lenin, *What Is To Be Done?* (Moscow), pp. 31, 78.

35. Arendt, 'On Violence' in her *Crises in the Republic* (Penguin), p. 99.

36. A weakness of Arendt's position is that she *counterposes* this aim to the aims of *social* revolution. What is required is a 'totalizing' approach which sees the political as a necessary aspect of a social revolution; and this in turn requires a non-reductionist concept of the social totality (see note 19, above).

37. Lenin, 'How to Organize Competition?', *Collected Works*, Vol. 26.

38. *Crises in the Republic*, p. 190.

39. Martin Jay, *The Dialectical Imagination* (Heinemann), pp. 57, 259; cf. *Dialectic of Enlightenment*, p. 41.

40. *Economic and Philosophic Manuscripts of 1844*, pp. 71–2.

41. *Capital*, Vol. I, p. 157.

42. *Grundrisse*, p. 84.

43. Ibid., p. 706.

44. On the production and reproduction of the relations of production, see Marx, *Grundrisse*, p. 458; *Capital*, Vol. I, p. 591; Vol. III, pp. 818, 879; and 'Immediate Results of the Process of Production', Appendix to Penguin edn. of *Capital*, Vol. I, p. 1065.

45. *Theses on Feuerbach*, VI.

46. *German Ideology*, p. 32.

47. Lobkowicz, op. cit., p. 9.

48. A. Labriola, *Essays on the Materialistic Conception of History* (Monthly Review Press), p. 228.

49. See further note 19, above. Althusser's explicit rejection of an anthropological grounding for the structure of the social totality may count as a further weakness in his position. At the very least I would maintain that Habermas raises important

issues for Marxists, and would therefore dissent from the sharply negative tone of Göran Therborn's in many ways useful discussion, 'Jürgen Habermas: A New Eclecticism', *New Left Review*, 67 (May–June 1971).

50. Hegel, *Phenomenology of Mind* (Allen & Unwin), pp. 229–40; the definitive commentary is Alexandre Kojève, *Introduction to the Reading of Hegel* (Basic Books). Hegel's emphasis on work or labour derives from a study of Adam Smith and the other political economists – see Lukács, *The Young Hegel* (Merlin Press), pp. 172, 319–37 – and it is thus no accident that 'Hegel's standpoint is that of modern political economy' (Marx, *1844 Manuscripts*, p. 140).

51. *Phenomenology*, p. 237.

52. *1844 Manuscripts*, p. 140.

53. See Habermas's discussion of labour and language in Hegel's Jena writings, *TP*, Ch. 4; some passages in which Hegel refers to language are cited below.

54. See Aristotle's *Ethics* (Penguin edn., pp. 303–9).

55. Feuerbach, *Principles of the Philosophy of the Future* (Bobbs-Merill), para. 62.

56. *Manuscripts*, p. 135; cf. Feuerbach, op. cit., para. 59. In *The German Ideology* (pp. 58–9; see also Engels' comments, pp. 659–60) Marx criticizes the passages here cited from Feuerbach; his argument is that though Feuerbach sees the relation of man to man as fundamental he grasps this relation and human nature itself in abstract and unhistorical terms. This of course does not mean that Marx rejects Feuerbach's positive insight, and when in the *Theses on Feuerbach*, VI, Marx maintains against Feuerbach that the human essence lies in 'the ensemble of the social relations' this should be understood as a development and concretization of Feuerbach's views, an immanent critique rather than a total break with him.

57. *Phenomenology*, p. 127 (I have drawn on Kaufmann's translation as well as Baillie's).

58. *1844 Manuscripts*, p. 95.

59. *German Ideology*, p. 42; note that a term Marx uses for 'relations of production' in *The German Ideology* is *Verkehrsverhaltnisse*, 'relations of intercourse'.

60. Ibid., p. 503.

61. *Phenomenology*, p. 660. Cf. Hegel, *Reason in History* (Bobbs-Merill), p. 78: 'Language is the work of theoretical intelligence in the true sense; it is its external expression.' See further his *Philosophy of Mind*, paras. 459, 462.

62. Engels, *Anti-Dühring* (Lawrence & Wishart), p. 333; the reference to Saint-Simon is on p. 307.

63. *Poverty of Philosophy*, p. 175; *Communist Manifesto* (Moscow), p. 76.

64. *Communist Manifesto*, loc. cit.

65. *Anti-Dühring*, loc. cit. Marx's view of the state is complex; he did not regard it merely as an instrument of class rule. But a more rounded treatment lies beyond the bounds of this paper.

66. In her 'On Violence' Arendt proposes a system of definitions designed to discriminate between *power* (which 'corresponds to the human ability not just to act but to act in concert') and *violence* (which she sees as distinguished by its 'instrumental character') (*Crises in the Republic*, pp. 113 ff. Cf. *HC*, p. 200.). She rejects the Leninist view that 'the most crucial political issue is . . . the question of Who rules Whom?'; her own belief is that we should cease to 'reduce public affairs to the business of dominion' (loc. cit.). Her system of definitions does indeed enable her to make some important points – e.g. 'No government exclusively based on the means of violence has ever existed' (p. 118; 'Rule by sheer violence comes into play

where power is being lost' (p. 121) – points which, for a Marxist, find their place in a theory of hegemony. However, Gramsci's concept of hegemony is valuable precisely because it relates questions of consent to power relations in the Leninist sense (Arendt's 'business of dominion'). Arendt's understanding of power as the human ability to act in concert in turn finds its place, for a Marxist, in the concept of the forces of production (which, as we have seen, encompass a 'practical' moment). For these reasons, in formulating my distinction between the two aspects or senses of politics, I have not followed Arendt's usage and have referred to one aspect – that which does not survive the withering away of the state – as the *power* dimension.

67. It is precluded by his linking of political power to knowledge, rigorously defined. Cf. Wolin, *Politics and Vision*, Ch. 2, and Arendt, *HC*, pp. 222–7. Arendt's argument is that Plato and, 'to a lesser degree', Aristotle himself saw political matters 'in the mode of fabrication', i.e. of 'work' (ibid., p. 230). Plato's exclusion of the interactive is, however, slightly modified by his comments on rhetoric at the end of the *Statesman* and his remarks on the need for preambles in the *Laws*.

68. These are central concepts in the political theory of Hobbes; Leo Strauss highlights them and relates the concept of fear in particular to Hegel's dialectic of Master and Slave – see his *The Political Philosophy of Hobbes* (University of Chicago Press), esp. pp. 57–8. See also Strauss's discussion of Hobbes in his *Natural Right and History* (University of Chicago Press), pp. 180 ff.

69. 'The Author as Producer', *New Left Review*, 62 (July–August 1970), p. 91; however, I would argue that the central thrust of this article, as of Brecht's aesthetics to which it relates, is towards a democratization of the technical on its own terms rather than towards the constitution of the specifically communicative or practical.

70. *Capital*, Vol. III, p. 820.

71. Roy Medvedev, *Let History Judge* (Spokesman Books), p. 239.

RE-THINKING THE 'BASE-AND-SUPERSTRUCTURE' METAPHOR

STUART HALL

Of the many problems which perforce Marx left in an 'undeveloped' state, none is more crucial than that of 'base-and-superstructure'. The manuscript of the third volume of *Capital* breaks off at the opening of the tantalizing passage on 'classes'. The promised volume on the State, which appears in several of the schemes for *Capital* which he prepared, was left unwritten. Both, if completed, would have thrown the light of his mature reflection on the base/superstructure question. As it is, we have a very substantial part of his mature thought on the 'laws of motion' of the capitalist mode of production, but nothing from the same period which takes as its theoretical object a capitalist social formation as a whole, encompassing all its levels and the relation between them, including the 'superstructures'.

There is a view that everything that Marxism needs is already there in *Capital*: and that, if you stare hard enough at it, it will – like the hidden books of the Bible – yield up all its secrets, a theory of everything. I don't subscribe to this thesis in its literal form. Apart from anything else, it denies one of the central premises of *Capital* – that the capitalist mode of production is constantly developing, and this in turn requires a continuous labour of theoretical development and clarification. 'There is no royal road to science', Marx warned the French (Preface to the French Edition of *Capital*, 1872: Marx, 1961). Besides, it smacks too much of the religious attitude. Of course, Marx's work on the laws of the capitalist mode of production contain many profound hints and pointers which await further theoretical development. What is more, *Capital* unravels the essential movements of that level which precisely Marx insisted was 'determining'. Hence, the problem of base/superstructure must be 'thought' within the terrain of concepts elaborated in that fundamental work. But it is a different proposition to imagine that it will be resolved by slavishly repeating the 'logic of *Capital*'. This too often results in an exercise which may be logically elegant, but is, in the larger theoretical sense, abstract: reducing everything to 'political economy'. To rethink the base/superstructure problem, within the framework of Marx's problematic as evidenced in *Capital*, requires difficult theoretical labour. This paper addresses itself, of necessity, to some starting points only.

What is fundamentally at issue here is: how does Marxism enable us to 'think' the complexities of a modern capitalist social formation? How can we conceptualize the relationships between the different levels which compose it? Further, can we 'think' this problem in such a way as to retain a key premise of historical materialism: the premise of 'determination in the last instance' by what is sometimes misleadingly referred to as 'the economic'? Can this be done without losing one's way in the idea of the *absolute* autonomy of each of its levels (for Marx insists that we must think the '*ensemble* of relations', its complex unity: and quoted with unqualified approval, in a text which Althusser unwarrantably defines as 'gestural', his Russian reviewer, who pointed to Marx's concern with 'that law of movement . . . which governs these phenomena, in so far as they have a definite form and mutual connexion within a given historical period' (*Afterword* to the second German edition of *Capital*)? Can it be done without succumbing to the notion of a capitalist social formation as a functional 'whole', without antagonism or contradiction ('The contradictions inherent in the movement of capitalist society . . . whose crowning point is the universal crisis' – Marx, *ibid*.)? Can it be done without falling back into the essentially relativistic sociological notion of a social formation as composed of a multivariate interaction-of-all-sides-on-one-another, without primacy of determination given or specified at any point? Can *determination* – one of the central themes of Marx's theoretical work – be thought without simplifying what it is that 'determines' (the economic?), when (in the last instance?) or how that determination operates (one-directionally)? In essence, those are the problems posed by the central position in Marxism occupied by the topographical metaphor of base/superstructure.

I want to look, briefly, at some of the key formulations in Marx and Engels' own work, which throw light on the base/superstructure question: noting not only the hints they throw out, but the developments in them and the shifts between them. Secondly, I examine one or two key developments in recent theoretical work which mark significant moments of further clarification; and attempt to estimate how far they take us, and what remains to be done.

The German Ideology

The first texts are taken from formulations offered in and around the period of the *German Ideology*. It is important to situate this text itself, and thus the conceptual field and the theoretical problematic in which the formulations are offered, This is the text where the 'species-being' perspective of the *Economic and Philosophical Manuscripts* is replaced, in often a simple but thorough-going manner, by a historical, often an evolutionary *genetic* materialism. It registers the 'break' with the problematic of Feuerbachean sensuous-materialism. It constitutes a 'settling of accounts', by Marx and Engels, with German 'critical criticism' – the speculative philosophy of the Left Hegelians. Its whole thrust – including its 'materialism' – is *polemical*. This polemical, reasonably simplifying, thrust of the text must be borne in mind if we are properly to situate the reductive simplifications which appear sometimes to intrude.

> The production of life, both of one's own by labour and of fresh life by procreation, appears at once as a double relationship, on the one hand as a natural on the other as a social relationship. By social is meant the cooperation of several individuals, no matter under what conditions, in what manner or to what end. It follows from this, that a determinate mode of production, or industrial stage, is always bound up with a determinate mode of cooperation or social stage, and this mode of cooperation is itself a 'productive force'. It also follows that the mass of productive forces accessible to men determines the condition of society, and that the 'history of humanity' must therefore always be studied and treated in relation to the history of industry and exchange.
>
> *(German Ideology)*

There are two key points to note here: both are restated in only a slightly different form at several other points in the text. The first is the proposition – the reverse of the Hegelian premise – that it is 'the mass of productive forces accessible to men' which 'determines the condition of society'. The second point is slightly more complex; but just as important. It just concerns the 'double relationship'. For Marx and Engels, 'men' (this is the general, historically undifferentiated, way in which people are referred to in this text) intervene in Nature in order to produce and reproduce their material conditions of life. This 'intervention' is accomplished through human labour and the use of tools. Human labour, ever since its first rudimentary historical appearance, is only possible through social co-operation between men: these 'relations', which develop between men, and constitute the 'determinate mode of co-operation', result from the historically specific mode of men's social intervention in Nature – their mode of production. The basis of all history is the successive modes of production, including the modes of social co-operation dependent on them. As Marx puts it in another similar passage: 'we are bound to study closely the men of the eleventh century and those of the eighteenth, to examine their respective needs, their productive forces, their mode of production, the raw materials of their production, and finally the relations of man to man which resulted from all these conditions of life' (*Poverty of Philosophy*, Marx, 1956). Each 'mode of production', each 'mode of cooperation' is 'determinate': historically specific. The latter 'results from' or 'is bound up with' the former. The premise of historical specificity in this relation between the two relations – the 'double relationship' – is insisted on throughout: but always in a very general, epochal, way. One way of measuring the distance – and the difference – between the Marx of this period and the Marx of *Capital* is precisely by comparing these general formulations with the chapters on 'Co-operation' and 'The Division Of Labour And Manufacture' in *Capital* I (Chs. XIII and XIV) to see how far the concept of historical specificity could itself be further specified.

The premises which inform these ways of attempting to 'expound' the relations between the different levels of a social formation are stated in an admirably simple and clear way, elsewhere in the same text. They constitute the working analytic principles of Marx's 'historical materialism', as this was developed by this point in time:

This conception of history, therefore, rests on the exposition of the real process of production, starting out from the simple material production of life and on the comprehension of the form of intercourse connected with and created by this mode of production, i.e. of civil society in its various stages as the basis of all history, and also in its action as the State. From this starting point, it explains all the different theoretical productions and forms of consciousness, religion, philosophy, ethics, etc., and traces their origins and growth, by which means the matter can of course be displayed as a whole (and consequently, also the reciprocal action of these various sides on one another). Unlike the idealist view of history, it does not to have look for a category in each period, but remains constantly on the real ground of history; it does not explain practice from the idea but explains the formation of ideas from material practice, and accordingly comes to the conclusion that all the forms of and products of consciousness can be dissolved, not by intellectual criticism, not by resolution into 'self-consciousness', or by transformation into 'apparitions', 'spectres', 'fancies', etc., but only by the practical overthrow of the actual social relations which gave rise to this idealist humbug; that not criticism but revolution is the driving force of history, as well as religion, philosophy, and all other types of theory.

(*German Ideology*, op. cit.)

The passage is too well known to require much comment. It contains the easily-recognized anti-Hegelian 'inversion': 'not practice from the idea but . . . the formation of ideas from material practice'. It begins to identify the different levels of a social formation. Note that these – constituting the germ of the base/superstructure metaphor – appear, if anything, as *three* levels, not two. The difference is important, even though the text, in its compression, tends to run them together. First, the 'material production of life . . . and the form of intercourse connected with and created by this mode of production'. Then – at, as it were, a different though related level of representation – 'i.e. civil society . . . and also its action as the State'. Then – another half distinction worth remarking: 'all the different theoretical productions and forms of consciousness, religion, philosophy, ethics, etc.' Note, here also, the variety of ways in which the principle of 'determination' is rendered: 'connected with'; 'created by'; 'in its action as'; etc.

The classic formulation, in its tightest and most succinct form, and clearly resting on the same conceptual terrain, appears again in the often quoted passage (but written nearly a decade later, and by a Marx already into his second draft, at least, of what is to become the first book of *Capital*): from the *Preface* of 1859 to the *Critique of Political Economy*, Marx, 1971) (replacing the longer, more complex, more theoretical and difficult Introduction to the *Grundrisse, of 1857*).

In the social production which men carry on they enter into definite relations that are indispensable and independent of their will; these relations of production correspond to a definite stage of development of their material powers of production. The totality of these relations of production constitutes the economic structure of society, the real foundation on which legal and political superstructure arise and to which definite forms of social consciousness correspond. The mode of production of material life determines the general character of the social, political, and spiritual processes of life. It is not the consciousness of men that determines their being, but, on the contrary, their social being determines their consciousness.

(Preface to *Critique of Political Economy*)

This clarifying but over-condensed paragraph contains all the elements of the base/superstructure problem as Marx formulated it in the middle, transitional period of his work up to the verge of the preparation of the first volume of *Capital*. Here, not only is material production and its relations the determining factor: but the 'corresponding' social relations are *given* – definite, indispensable and independent of men's will: objective conditions of a social mode of production. These, under determinate conditions, constitute a *stage*. This – material mode, relations of production is what is designated as 'the economic structure'. It forms the base, the 'real foundation'. From it arise the legal and political superstructures. And, *to this* correspond theoretical productions *and* definite forms of social consciousness.

Marx's 'Historicism'

The formulations in both the *German Ideology* and the 1859 *Preface* clearly exhibit what would now be identified as the traces of Marx's *historicism*. That is to say, a determining primacy is given to the base – basis, real foundation – and the other levels of a social formation are seen to develop in close correspondence with it: even if this is not phrased uni-directionally ('and consequently, also, the reciprocal action of these various sides on one another'); and even if changes at one level are subject to a time-lag at the other levels ('the entire immense superstructure is *more or less rapidly* transformed'). The 'matter which is displayed as a whole' is thought in terms of a broad determination; changes in the economic structure of society will, 'more or less rapidly', produce consequent and determinate changes in the legal and political superstructures and in the 'ideological forms in which men become conscious of this conflict and fight it out' – that is, also, at the ideological level.

Althusser would argue that, here, the social totality is conceptualized, essentially, as an 'expressive totality'; in which, despite its apparent levels and differentiations, contradictions in the 'base' appear to unroll, evenly, and to be reflected sooner or later through corresponding modifications in the superstructures and the ideological forms. This, then, is still an 'essentialist' conceptualization of a social formation. It is also 'historicist', in Althusser's view, because it makes little if any separation between 'theoretical productions' and 'ideological forms'; it makes the theoretical level appear also as a 'correspondence' or a reflection of the material base.

We shall return to the weight and force of this critique of the 'historicist' Marx, at a later point. But, in the work of Althusser, the *German Ideology* is presented as the work of a 'break' and 'transitional' period in Marx's work (cf. *For Marx*, p. 197); to be superseded, in *Capital*, by a transformed dialectic, which produces an altogether different manner of conceptualizing a social formation. It is therefore worth noting *where* and *how* this earlier formulation (which, appearing as it does in the 1859 *Preface*, comes relatively very late in the so-called epistemological rupture between the early and middle Marx, and the 'late') reappears again in Marx's mature work.

In a passage in *Capital* III, Marx offers an interesting and important gloss, which is, however, different, from the *German Ideology*, above all in the tightness of its formulation:

> The specific economic form in which unpaid surplus labour is pumped out of the direct producers determines the relation of domination and servitude, as it emerges directly out of production itself and in its turn reacts upon production. Upon this basis, however, is founded the entire structure of the economic community, which grows up out of the conditions of production itself, and consequently its specific political form. It is always the direct relation between the masters of the conditions of production and the direct producers which reveals the innermost secret, the hidden foundation of the entire social edifice, and therefore also of the political form of the relation between sovereignty and dependence, in short, of the particular form of the State.
>
> (Mark, *Capital* III)

Here it is the relations of 'domination and servitude', defined far more specifically in terms of the way surplus value is extracted in capitalist production, which 'reveals the innermost secret, the hidden foundations of the entire social edifice'; hence, its political forms; and thus the forms of the state itself. In another, more significant, passage, Marx quotes his own words from the 1859 *Preface* in a long and important footnote in the chapter on 'Commodities' in *Capital* I. He quotes it without modification – and clearly with approval. The context and development is, however, also significant. A German critic had quoted Marx's 1859 *Preface*: and, while acknowledging the primacy of 'the economic' in the capitalist epoch, denied its determining role for the feudal period or for classical antiquity, 'where politics reigned supreme'. Marx, in reply, restates the basic premise: it is 'the economic structure' which is 'the real basis'. (We must remember, however, that whereas this 'structure' is treated in a very reduced and simple form in the original formulation, it is now recalled in the context of a work which is devoted to an extremely comprehensive and elaborate consideration of just what the forms and relations of this 'structure' are). The middle ages, he continues, could not live on Catholicism nor Ancient Rome on politics.

However, he adds, 'it is the mode in which they gained a livelihood which explains why here politics and there Catholicism played the chief part' (*Capital* I, p. 82). Thus, while the mode of production plays a determining role in all epochs, its role appears here as that of assigning to some *other* level of practice (politics, religion – i.e. ideology) the 'chief role' (the *dominant* role, as it has come to be designated). This is a new way of formulating the problem of 'determination by the economic' – and one which, incidentally, gives far greater effectivity to the 'superstructures' (which can now, in some epochs, be dominant). The argument is already anticipated in the 1857 *Introduction*, where Marx argues that 'In all forms of society there is one specific kind of production which predominates over the rest whose relations thus assign rank and influence to the others. . . . It is a particular ether which determines the specific gravity of every being which has materialised within it' (Marx, *Grundrisse*).

These are, of course two of the principal sources for the Althusserean distinction between 'determining' and 'dominant' instances: and thus for the thesis that, in his later work, Marx ceased to think a social formation as a simple expressive totality. We will return to this important turn in the argument later.

The crucial formulations of the base/superstructure problem first occur, and are given at least one decisive, and quite consistent form, in the period between the consignment of the *German Ideology* to the 'gnawing criticism of the mice' and the replacement of the 1857 *Introduction* by the 1859 *Preface*. Whether later superseded and transformed or not, these formulations give a radical impetus to the whole body of Marxist thought on the question of how to conceptualize a social formation and how to 'explore' the nature of its unity. Let us sum it up.

The texts here are reformulated in the problematic of a broad, epochal historical sweep. In this sweep, mode of production is given, first, its initial definition; secondly, its position of determination over the whole social edifice and structure. Mode of production is already conceptualized as consisting, neither of economic relations *per se*, nor of anything so vulgarly material as 'level of technology': but as a combination of relations – productive forces, social relations of production. These, in each epoch, form the determining matrix, in which social life and material existence is produced and reproduced. And the structures raised on this foundation, which embody and articulate the social relations stemming from the productive matrix, correspond to it. Indeed, in the 'double relationship', both – material and social reproduction – are simultaneously founded. As men, through the division of labour, progressively combine to intervene, by means of the developing forces of production, in Nature to reproduce their material life, so they in the same moment reproduce the structure of their social relations, and reproduce themselves as social individuals. The two cannot be separated, even if, in the last instance, it is the former which determines the form of the latter. Indeed, this 'double relation' is conceptualized as *asymptotic*: since, in production, the social relations themselves progressively become 'a productive force'. As these social relations, rooted in and governed by production develop, they achieve a distinct articulation: they are embodied in political and legal relations. They give rise to determinate forms of the State ('The existing relations of production must necessarily express themselves also as political and legal relations'). They define the character of civil society ('Only in the 8th Century, in "civil society", do the various forms of social connectedness confront the individual as a mere means towards his private purposes, as external necessity' – 1857 *Introduction*). They produce their corresponding theoretical fields and discourses (religion, ethics, philosophy, etc.) and 'determinate forms of social consciousness' ('that these concepts are accepted as mysterious powers is a necessary consequence of the independent existence assumed by the real relations whose expressions they are'). This is, indeed, the point towards which the whole trajectory of the *German Ideology* tended – the setting of the feet of German idealist speculation in the soil of man's 'profane history'.

No simple or reductive reflexivity of the superstructures is assumed here, though the *thrust* behind the many reformulations is consistent, and unmistakable. And perhaps it is worth stressing that, if Marx's thought on the subject subsequently developed, what changed is *how* he came to understand determinacy by a mode of production, not whether it determined or not. When we leave the terrain of 'determinations', we desert, not just this or that stage in Marx's thought, but his whole problematic. It is also worth noting that, though the determinacy of 'the economic' over the superstructures is the prevailing form in which this is expressed here, it is sometimes overlaid by a second template: the tendency to reduce determination, not to 'the economic' but to History itself – to *praxis*: to an undifferentiated *praxis* which rolls throughout the whole social formation, as its essential ground. Some passages of the *German Ideology* are not all that far from the more humanist-historicist assertion of the *Holy Family* that 'History is nothing but the activity of men.' Succint as are its formulations, then, the *German Ideology* remains, at one and the same time, a key early text of historical materialism, *and* a text haunted or shadowed by the trace of more than one conceptual problematic.

Engels's letters on historical materialism

One of the best ways of seeing what the problems were for Marxism of the 'German Ideology' way of conceptualizing the base/super-structure question, is to watch Engels wrestle with its consequences in his lengthy correspondence with a number of Marxist veterans of his and the next generation, in the two decades after Marx's death. (Cf. the Correspondence, in Marx–Engels *Selected Works*, Vol. 2, 1951.) In addition to editing and bringing together Marx's vast unpublished work, Engels found himself both the guardian of his and Marx's joint legacy, and its most privileged interpreter. This was a key moment, and role, for it 'marked the transition, so to speak, from Marx to Marxism and provided the formative moment of all the leading Marxist interpreters of the Second International and most of the leaders of the Third' (Stedman Jones, *New Left Review*, 79, 1973). Marx had laid the foundations, above all in his work on the capitalist mode of production. But he left 'no comparable *political* theory of the structures of the bourgeois State, or of the strategy and tactics of revolutionary socialist struggle by a working-class party for its overthrow' (Anderson, *Considerations on Western Marxism*, 1976). Nor did he provide any systematic general statement of historical materialism as a 'world view'. Engels attempted to repair both omissions – a task which gives the general sense 'of a completion, more than a development, of Marx's heritage' (Anderson, op. cit.).

Marx had established that the economy is determinant in the last instant, but that the superstructures had their own 'effectivity' which could not be simply reduced to their base. But 'the precise structural mechanism connecting the two is always left unclear by Marx' (Stedman Jones, op. cit.). The clarification of this problem was one of Engels's most urgent and important tasks: the more so since Marxism was fast becoming absorbed into the dominant field of 'positive science', which reduced it to a simple economic determinism in which the superstructures were a pale and automatic reflex of the base – a tendency which was destined to be disastrously installed as the official version in the Second International. Engels struggled vainly to combat this reductionism. But he struggled to do so on the ground, essentially, of his and Marx's formulations of the *German Ideology* period: and the development and clarification he undertook were sustained by precisely those conceptual tools and instruments which had produced the formulation in this form in the first place. That is, *essentially* as an inversion of the idealist premises left intact in Left Hegelianism – by setting the Hegelian dialectic right-side-up, and working from its 'revolutionary' aspect. In the letters, Engels wrestles with this inheritance valiantly, courageously and often elegantly. But the conceptual chickens are fast coming home to roost.

The *German Ideology* proposed a general historical scheme: but now that this threatened to harden into a rigid and abstract orthodoxy, Engels was obliged to insist that 'All history must be studied afresh' and that Marx's materialism is 'not a lever for construction à la Hegelianism' (letter to Carl Schmidt, 5/8/1890). Face to face with 'determination by the economic', Engels has to win some space for the 'interaction of all these elements', and for the 'endless host of accidents' through which 'the economic movement finally asserts itself as necessary' (Engels to J. Bloch, 21–22/9/1890). He accepts some blame ('Marx and I are ourselves partly to blame . . .') for the tendency to reduce everything to the economic, and to disregard the effect of the superstructures and the ideological forms in 'exercising their influence upon the course of the historical struggles'. The play between contingency and necessity, the 'infinite series of parallelograms of forces which give rise to one resultant', the intersection of many individual wills into 'a collective mean, a common resultant' are bold and provocative attempts to circumvent some of the problems implicit in the original problematic (cf. letter to Bloch). There are some useful and provocative advances made in Engels's long, detailed letter to Schmidt (27/10/1876), which deal specifically with the superstructural instances of the Law and the State, which are worth pursuing in a later context.

But we cannot depart far from Althusser's judgement on this correspondence, in the lucid Appendix to his 'Contradiction and Overdetermination' essay (*For Marx*), which suggests that, despite their many strengths, Engels's attempts to find a theoretical solution in the Correspondence principally have the result of declaring that a solution is not yet to hand, and of reminding us how difficult it is to find. The problem, Althusser suggests, is: how to think the specific relations between the relations of production and the political, juridical and ideological forms in such a way as to grasp, simultaneously, the 'determination by the economic in the last instance' and the 'relative autonomy' or effectivity of the superstructures. Engels knows what the question is: but he does not produce a satisfactory solution to it.

We have traced the 'after-life' of the *German Ideology* formulations beyond Marx's death, partly as a way of registering the continuing theoretical power and resonance which they still – and in a sense, must – carry within the Marxist tradition. But the fact is that they were beginning to be superseded and transformed, implicitly if not explicitly, and in terms of the bringing into use of the elements of an alternative paradigm, even if not 'fully theorized', within Marx's own lifetime and within the scope of his later work. We can identify three ways or directions in which this modification is taking place.

The first is to be found in the political writings – above all, the *Eighteenth Brumaire*, the *Class Struggles in France* and the more incidental notes on Britain – which Marx wrote after it became clear that the revolutions of 1848 were not destined to produce a swift resolution to the emerging proletarian struggles (cf. *Surveys From Exile*, and D. Fernbach's excellent introduction; 1973). In these writings Marx is not only dealing with concrete social formations at a specific historical moment, but his attention is focused on one level of the superstructure – the *political* instance. Hence, though these writings contain no general theoretical reformulations, they contain essential insights into how, in detail, Marx thought of the 'effectivity of the superstructures'.

Second, there are Marx's cryptic Notes at the end of the 1857

Introduction, tantalizingly headed 'Forms of the State and Forms of Consciousness in Relation to Relations of Production and Circulation. Legal Relations. Family Relations'. These are too epigramatic and condensed to help us much. But they point to Marx's recognition of the difficulty; and they contain the crucial, if cryptic, identification of the 'law of uneven development'.

Third, there is, of course, the whole monumental theoretical edifice of *Capital* itself. There is no extensive passage, as we have said, in *Capital* in which the 'laws of motion of the capitalist mode of production' are extended into the other levels of a social formation. But there are absolutely pivotal indications and traces of how this might be done, on the basis of Marx's decipherment of capital's secret. These do not add up to a thorough reworking of the base/superstructure problem. But they do, in sum, constitute an important, if incomplete, reflexive theoretical clarification.

The Eighteenth Brumaire

Before briefly looking at each of these moments, in turn, we can usefully sum up here the direction in which this incomplete clarification points. Crudely put, the relation of base to superstructure is thought, in the *German Ideology*, as some kind of fairly direct or immediate correspondence – i.e. within the framework of an *identity* theory. Marx progressively criticizes and departs from identity theory. Essentially, two things provoke this 'break'. Historically, the antagonisms multiplying at the economic level, fail, in the revolutions of 1848, to produce their 'corresponding' political resolutions. Marx is therefore forced, not only to abandon the perspective of 'immediate catastrophe' which had been ringingly tolled out in the *Communist Manifesto*, but to look again at the much more complex inter-play between the political and the economic; and to consider the ways in which 'solutions' could be found, at the political level, which thwarted, modified or even displaced the contradictions accumulating at the economic level – taking them forward, in their contradictory form, to a higher level of development.

The *Eighteenth Brumaire* is the classic instance of such an analysis of the 'effectivity' and specificity of the political instance in relation to the economic. 'Here Marx began, for the first time, to develop a systematic set of concepts for coming to grips with the phenomena of a politics which is certainly that of class struggle – the struggle of groups whose existence and interests are defined by the relations of production – but which is nevertheless *politics*, practised in the field of ideology and coercion that gives it its specific character' (Fernbach, Introduction to *Surveys From Exile*). This is the direct result of a longer and more complex perspective, born in the failed dénouement of 1848. Gwyn Williams has recently brilliantly expounded, from an *internal* reading of the *Eighteenth Brumaire*, precisely how and where this historical 'break' registers as an analytic 'break' inside Marx's text (cf. Open University, The Revolution of 1848, Unit A321, 5/6/7/8, on *France*). Engels subsequently remarked that in 1848, he and Marx had mistaken the *birth-pangs* of capitalism for its *death-throes*.

But the break is also provoked theoretically. For the more Marx examined in depth the capitalist mode of production, the more he observed the internal complexities of its laws and relations: and the less he thought this complex whole could be expounded in terms of the immediate correspondence between one of its circuits and another, let alone one of its levels and all the others. This major revision is of course practically exemplified in the conceptual structure of *Capital* itself. But it is also stated, as a matter of theory and method, in the 1857 *Introduction*, which contains a thorough critique of 'identity theory' and begins to sketch out a Marxist alternative – a theory of *articulations* between relations which are in no sense immediately corresponding. We cannot examine this here, but it provides, so to speak, the pivotal transitional point between the *German Ideology* and *Capital* itself. (cf. Hall, 'Notes on Marx's method', in *WPCS* 6, 1974.)

Thus, in this period, Marx's 'clarification' turns our attention in a new direction. He is concerned, now, with the *necessary complexity* of the social formations of advancing capitalism and of the relations between its different levels. He is concerned with the 'unevenness', the non-immediate correspondences, between these levels which remain, nevertheless, connected. He is concerned with the functions which, specifically, the superstructures 'perform' in relation either to the maintenance and reproduction, or the retardation of the development, of capitalist social relations: and with the fact that these functions not only appear in ever-more complex forms, but that, at a certain stage of their development, may actually *require* the non-immediacy – the 'relative autonomy' – they exhibit. This is a different problematic from that of the *German Ideology* period. It is also different from Engels's attempts to extend the chain of reflexivity between base and superstructures, in a simple, linear way (in the Correspondence especially: elsewhere, as we shall suggest, Engels contributes some useful insights for Marx's new problematic).

Before looking, briefly, at the *Eighteenth Brumaire*, his most 'worked' example, we can pinpoint from a number of sources the problems which constitute the field of Marx's new problematic.

When Marx examined British politics in the series of articles for the *New York Daily Tribune* which he commenced in 1852, he had to confront the stubborn fact that, though the capitalist mode of production was fast developing, and with it an emergent industrial bourgeoisie, the latter appeared to 'rule' either through a Tory party, representing the large landed proprietors, or through the Whig party, consisting of 'the oldest, richest, and most arrogant portion of English landed property' . . . 'the aristocratic representatives . . . of the industrial and commercial middle class'. To them, apparently, the bourgeoisie had abandoned the 'monopoly of government and the exclusive possession of office'. How capital advanced through this complex political configuration – giving rise to a distinction between an 'economically ruling class' and, at the level of the political superstructures, a 'politically governing caste' – was a fundamental problem; for the dynamic of British politics (and the politics of the working class, which remained tied to the tail of the Whig–Radical alliance) was constantly mediated – deflected – through its structure. In fact, as Fernbach notes, Marx understood Britain politically far less well than France. He never grasped the deep compromise on which, after the settlement, British political life was stabilized; and he believed that ultimately, the industrial bourgeoisie would transform everything in its wake and assume power directly, 'battering Old England to pieces'. In fact, 'the industrial bourgeoisie managed to integrate itself politically and culturally into the old ruling bloc and the aristocratic "mask" was to remain for at least a further half-century to camouflage and mystify the rule of capital' (Fernbach, op. cit.). But, if Marx mistook the line of development, he was not wrong in locating the issue: an issue, essentially, of non-identity between the classes in dominance at the economic level and the class factions in power, at the level of politics and the State. (Cf. on this problem, the extended controversy between Anderson, Nairn and Thompson.)

Take another superstructural domain. In his *Critique of Hegel's Philosophy of Law*, Marx noted that the Law served 'to perpetuate a particular mode of production'; yet insisted that 'the influence exercised by laws on the preservation of existing conditions of distribution, and the effect they thereby exert on production, has to be examined *separately*'. Engels echoed this sentiment when, in *Feuerbach and The End Of Classical German Philosophy* (*MESW*, 1951), in a long and interesting section on the state, law and ideology, he shows how England retained the forms of the old feudal law, whilst giving them a bourgeois content; how Roman Law provided the foundation for the evolution of bourgeois legal relations elsewhere; how this 'working up into a special code of law' proved to be a poor basis for the development of Prussia, but − transformed into the *Code Civil* − an extremely favourable one for France. Thus, though 'bourgeois legal rules merely express' the economic life conditions of society in legal form, they can do so well or ill according to circumstances. In the same passage, Engels notes how, to achieve articulation as a sphere of the superstructure, economic facts must 'assume the form of juristic motives', thereby leading on to the formation of a fully-fledged juridical sphere, a set of complex legal ideologies, with an efficacy of their own. 'It is indeed among professional politicians, theorists of public law and jurists of private law that the connection with the economic facts gets really lost.' It is, then, not surprising that it is in relation to legal relations that Marx states his 'law of uneven development' in the *Grundrisse*: 'But the really difficult point to discuss here is how relations of production develop *unevenly* as legal relations. Thus, e.g. the relation of Roman private law . . . to modern production.' There seems little doubt that, had this point been expanded by Marx at the length of, say, Book One of *Capital*, the one thing it would *not* have exhibited is a simple law of correspondence between the material base and the forms of the superstructure.

The *Eighteenth Brumaire* is, then, relatively simple to set in this context of problems − though its argument is not simple either to follow or resume. It concerns, essentially, the relation of the politics of the 1851 crisis in France, the forms of political regime and of the State which emerge, the nature of the Bonapartist 'solution', and, more incidentally, the basis of ideology − 'Napoleon's ideas' − in the accumulating contradictions generated by the development of an industrial capitalist mode of production. The latter is, however, here refracted through the former: it is the political instance which is in the foreground, just as, in 1851, it was politics which 'took command'. The

French mode of production is beginning to develop, throwing up its antagonisms: the class fractions related to this development are already, politically, on stage: but so are those fractions which represent continuing, if declining modes of production still coexisting with industrial capital in the French social formation (the fact that the political complexity of the moment of 1851 is related to the coexistence of modes of production, with no single mode as yet in full dominance, is a crucial step in the argument). In one sense, then, the political crisis of 1851 is *given* at the level of mode of production. It may even be seen that, in a long-term sense, the stage of development (i.e. under-development) of the capitalist mode of production is what prescribes – determines, in an epochal sense – the *range* of 'solutions' to the crisis possible at this stage of development (i.e. no clear resolutions, one way or another). What it certainly does *not* do is to prescribe, in detail, either the content or forms of the political conjuncture. The December crisis runs through a succession of different regimes, each representing a shifting coalition of class fractions. Daily, the political content of the Napoleonic state shifted – formed and dissolved. Each coalition temporarily gave rise to a succession of forms of regime: social republic, democratic republic, parliamentary republic. It is only as each exhausts its possibilities of hegemony, and is dissolved, since none can rule the whole social formation on its own, that the Bonapartist 'solution' is prepared: the *coup d'état*. This is a regressive moment, from the point of view of capital, arresting its development. France 'seems to have escaped the despotism of a class only to fall back beneath the despotism of one individual' (*18th Brumaire*, MESW, 1951). The falling of France on its face before the rifle butt of Louis-Napoleon's troops corresponds to the 'backwardness' of the French mode of production – and ensures that backwardness for a period. The lack of resolution – the situation of almost perfect equilibrium between the various contending fractions, leaving room for none definitively to prevail – provides the conditions in which the State itself appears, as a neutral structure 'above the contending classes', and enormously expands its range and 'autonomy'. Finally, Louis-Napoleon's regime – which appears in the form of a single despotism – in fact is seated on the back of a particular class interest: that of the 'most numerous' class in France at that moment, though one destined to decline – the small-holding peasantry. This class fraction cannot rule in its own name: it rules *through* Napoleon and through his ideas. It is this class which temporarily gives content to the expanding State – for the State is not 'suspended in mid-air': but Louis-Napoleon, revivifying spirits, names, battle cries and costumes from the past (the past of another and greater Napoleon), is the *conductor* of the power of this class to the political level. Capital settles for a 'postponement'. 'Bonapartism' is its name and form.

Without examining this argument in any further detail, it should be sufficient to see from this and the related essays of this period, that the domain of the political/juridical superstructures and the forms of the State itself are no longer thought by Marx as in any simple reflexive or expressive sense corresponding to their base. In the development of a Marxist theory of the superstructures, this essay must occupy a *pivotal position* (as it did for Gramsci, one of the major contributors to such a theory).

Re-reading 'Capital'

We have suggested that, properly understood, there are hints in the structure of the argument in *Capital* about how this new problematic of base and superstructure can be developed, as well, of course, as a major exposition of the necessary conceptual ground on which this theoretical development should be undertaken. There is no space to take this very far here. One way is to take the law and tendencies of 'the self-expansion of capital', not as specifying in detail the content and forms of the superstructures and thereby 'determining', but as providing the governing movements (including the contradictions and crises in that self-expansion, and the 'solutions' which permit capital to continue to accumulate while reproducing its antagonisms at a more advanced level of composition), dictating the tempo and rhythms of development in the other parts of the social formation: setting limits, as it were, to what can or cannot be a solution adaptable to capital's self-expanding needs, and thus as determining through the *repertoire* of solutions (political, social, ideological) likely to be drawn on in any particular historical moment or conjuncture.

This involves a 'reading' – some would say *another* 'reading' – of *Capital*, treating it neither as the theoretical analysis of a 'pure' mode of production (whatever that is), nor as a history of British capitalism in the nineteenth century, which seem at this point in time to be the two prevailing alternatives on offer. We would have to try, instead, to understand, for example, as Marx does, the shift from the extraction of absolute to the extraction of *relative* surplus value as one of the key dynamics of the developing capitalist mode of production; as not merely a theoretical distinction but one which can be made concrete and historically specific in, say, the capitalist mode in England after the factory legislation of the mid-century. We can then see this shift as providing the base-line of solutions to the contradictions to which capitalism, as a fully established mode of production, is progressively exposed. If we then attempt to think all that is involved – politically, socially, ideologically, in terms of the State, of politics, of the reproduction of skills, of the degree of labour and the application of science as a 'productive force', as a consequence of the uneven development towards this second 'moment' in the unfolding of capitalist accumulation (i.e. as the inner spark which prompts many of the transformations in capitalism which we now sum up as the 'transition from laissez-faire to monopoly') – then, we begin to see how *Capital* provides a foundation for the development of a Marxist theory of the superstructures within the framework of 'determination in the last instance'; without falling back into the identity-correspondence position outlined in the *German Ideology*.

That is, so to speak, re-examining the base/superstructure problem from the perspective of 'the base'. But it is also possible, within the framework of *Capital*, to reconstruct certain key mechanisms and tendencies of the superstructures from distinctions Marx is always drawing between the 'base' levels of production and exchange. And this helps us to understand how it can be possible to insist that, within Marxism, the superstructures are at one and the same moment 'determined' and yet absolutely, fundamentally necessary and required: not empty ideological forms and illusions. This relates to what is now sometimes called the theory of *Darstellung* or 'representation' in Marx (cf. Althusser and Balibar, *Reading Capital*, 1970; Geras, 1971; Mepham, *WPCS* 6, 1974; Glucksmann, 1972; Callinicos, 1976). Without taking on a complex account of this theory here, we may try to approach it more easily through Marx's notion or concept of *appearances* (and thus to the theory of 'fetishism' as outlined in *Capital* I, Part 1; though there is considerable argument as to whether the theories of *Darstellung* and the theory of 'fetishism' are in fact the same).

Often, though by no means exclusively, the question of appearances or of 'real relations'/'phenomenal forms' is linked, in *Capital*, with the distinction between production and exchange. In the 1857 *Introduction* and throughout *Capital*, Marx insists on the necessary relation between the circuits of exchange (where value is realized) and the conditions pertaining to it, and the circuits of capital through production and the conditions pertaining to that. These, he says, must not be thought of as 'identical'. They are complementary but different; articulated with each other, but each still requiring its own conditions to be sustained. Hence the 'unity' which these processes exhibit is not a unity of identity, but 'unity of the diverse' – the 'concentration of many determinations'. Now, though these processes remain linked in their differences, and each is necessary for the 'self-expansion and realization of value', production is the determining level: 'consumption appears as a moment of production'. The sphere of exchange is, however, what *appears* to dominate, to provide the 'real' level of social relations under capitalism: it is also the sphere in which the myriad everyday 'exchanges' of capitalist market relations take place, dictated only by the hidden but miraculous hand of the market. It is thus the sphere of capitalism's 'common sense' – that is, where our spontaneous and everyday common-sense perceptions and experiences of the system arises: and it is also the starting point of bourgeois theory – both vulgar political economy, and after that, marginal economics deal principally with the domain of circulation.

Now, all the relations of the sphere of exchange really exist – they are not figments of anyone's imagination. Value could not be realized without them. There is a labour market, where labour power is bought and sold – the form of the contract being the wage. There are markets in which commodities exchange against money – the form of the contract being prices. This sphere of 'free exchange', where labour appears to exchange against its 'due price' (a 'fair wage') and where goods appear to exchange at their equivalences (real prices) is the domain of private egoistic exchanges which political economy named 'civil society'. To put it briefly, and in a very simplified form, Marx argues two things about this sphere of capitalist society. Looking – to use a special metaphor – 'downwards', this sphere conceals the real, but highly unequal and exploitative relations of production. The concentration on, indeed the *fetishization* of, the sphere of exchange *masks* what founds it and makes it possible: the generation and extraction of the surplus in the sphere of capitalist production. Thus, at the level of exchange, the agents of the process appear as one individual confronting another: whereas, of course, this epoch of egoistic individuals 'which produces this standpoint, that of the isolated individual, is also precisely that of the hitherto most developed *social . . .* relations' (*Grundrisse*). Thus, when the production relations of capitalism *appear as* (and are treated, conceptually as consisting of nothing except) exchange relations, the effect of this re-presentation is to mask and occlude what the 'real relations' of capitalism are. This is the theory of representation, and it is also part of the theory of 'fetishism'. It indicates why Marx is so insistent throughout *Capital* on the difference between 'real relations' and their 'phenomenal forms' – without his entertaining for a moment the idea that the 'phenomenal forms' are imaginary or do not exist.

However, looking – to use the spatial metaphor again – 'upwards', Marx then notes that it is these phenomenal relations which constitute the basis of civil society and the politico-juridical relations: that is, the superstructures. And from that level, also, arise the various forms of ideological consciousness. '*On the surface* of bourgeois society', Marx writes, 'the wage of the labourer *appears as* the price of labour, a certain quantity of money that is paid for a certain quantity of labour' . . . 'This phenomenal form which makes the actual relation invisible and indeed shows the direct opposite of that relation forms the basis of all the *juridical notions* of both labourer and capitalist, of all the mystifications of the capitalist mode of production, of all its illusions as to *liberty*, of all the apologetic shifts of the *vulgar economists*' . . . 'The exchange between capital and labour at first *presents itself* to the mind in the same guise as the buying and selling of all other commodities', he adds a little further on. Finally, he concludes, 'The former [the "phenomenal form"] appear directly and spontaneously *as current modes of thought*: the latter [the real relations] must first be discovered by science.' (All these quotes from the Chapter XIX on 'Wages', in *Capital* I. Our italics. The formulations are recapitulated again and again through this volume.) Thus, he says elsewhere, in a famous passage at the end of Part II of *Capital*, 'we . . . take leave for a time of this noisy sphere where everything takes place on the surface and in view of all men, and follow them . . . to the hidden abode of production. . . . This sphere that we are deserting, within whose boundaries the sale and purchase of labour-power goes on, is in fact a very Eden of the innate rights of man. There alone rule Freedom, Equality, Property and Bentham. Freedom, because both buyer and seller of a commodity, say, labour power, are constrained only by their free will. They contract as free agents, and the agreement they come to is but the form in which they give legal expression to their common will . . .'. Those who would like to found a theory of the superstructures, and the ideological discourses and spontaneous common-sense notions which fill out and help to organize the terrain of the superstructures, and who wish nevertheless to know how *and why* these emerge, in determinate forms, from the level of a mode of production, have, it seems to me, little or no alternative but to begin to work outwards from this essential starting point at the heart of the argument in the mature Marx in *Capital* itself. (For an elaboration of this starting point, cf: Geras, 1972; Mepham, 1974; Hall, 1975.)

Gramsci

The problem of base/superstructure has been the subject of considerable further development and theorizing, especially within 'Western Marxism' – though it must be said that few appear to try to work *outwards* from the terrain of the mature Marx in the way tentatively formulated above. Most attempts have preferred to go back to the less adequate formulations of the *German Ideology* period. What is more, many of these attempts have been concerned with the specifically *ideological* dimensions of the superstructures. We have neglected this aspect here, not only because it has been much written about, and because it constitutes a difficult area of theorizing in itself, but also because the concentration on the problems of ideology has, until recently, obscured the fact that when Marx refers to the superstructures, he is discussing the forms, relations and apparatuses of the State and civil society, *as well as* the 'ideological forms and forms of social consciousness corresponding to them'. Since Lenin and Gramsci – until Poulantzas and Althusser placed the problem once more squarely on the agenda – the superstructures in the true Marxian sense, including the absolutely critical question of the nature of the capitalist State, have been woefully neglected.

In the space left at our disposal, only two positions can, even cursorily, be considered. They constitute, however, in our view, the really significant contribution, post Marx, Engels and Lenin, to the development of a Marxist 'theory of the superstructures' and of the base/superstructure relation.

The first contributor here is Gramsci. Gramsci's work was undertaken first in the very centre of the great upsurge of proletarian struggle in Italy in the immediately post-First World War period, and then continued, under the most difficult circumstances of imprisonment. Gramsci was forced to ponder long and hard the difficult question of how Marxism could inform revolutionary political practice. He was also forced, by the 'exceptional' nature of the Italian State, to consider deeply the question of the nature of the capitalist State in both its 'normal' and its exceptional forms (it was one of those exceptions, after all – the fascist State of Mussolini – which put him behind bars). He was also, as a result of his Crocean early training, peculiarly alerted to the enlarging or (as Croce put it) 'ethical' functions of the State, and what this concept would mean when translated into Marxist terms. And he was involved, as one of the leading militants in the international communist movement, directly with the same problems which had precipitated Lenin's fundamental text, *State and Revolution*.

It is not possible to recapitulate Gramsci's formulations about the State and the superstructures here. All that we can do is to indicate the *direction* of Gramsci's thinking in this domain. Much of Gramsci's work is directed in polemic against economic reductive theories of the superstructures. Hence he argued that the proper posing of the relation between base and superstructures was the seminal issue in a Marxist theory of politics ('The Modern Prince', in *Prison Notebooks*, 1971). Fundamental class relations always, under conditions of developing capitalist relations, extend themselves in and through the 'complex spheres of the superstructures'; for only thus could the reproduction of the social relations of capitalism be carried through in such a way as, progressively, to draw civil, social, political and cultural life into a larger conformity with capital and its needs. In developed capitalist social formations, this *englargement* of capital's sway throughout the social formation as a whole depended, precisely, on the development of the State and of civil society. Here, Gramsci paid close attention to the 'ethical' function of the State, by which he meant the 'work' which the State performs on behalf of capital in establishing a new level of civilization, creating a new kind of social individual appropriate to the new levels of material existence accomplished by the development of capitalism's base. It was through the State, through its work in and with the family, the law, education, the multiplicity of private associations, the cultural apparatus, the church, the formation of new strata of the intelligentsia, the formation of political parties and the development of public opinion – in short, in the complex sphere of the superstructures – that capitalism ceased to be simply a system of production and became a whole form of social life, conforming everything else to its own movement. This expansion of the conception of what it is the superstructures 'do' for capital is Gramsci's first contribution.

The second is the manner in which he generates those critical intermediary concepts which enable us to think the *specificity* of a superstructural level. Here we have in mind Gramsci's development of the political instance, and the critical (if often provisional and cryptic) concepts he elaborates there of 'relations of force', hegemony, historical bloc, corporate and subaltern classes, class fractions, Caesarism, Bonapartism, etc. Once again, in Gramsci's concept of 'hegemony', for example, we discover the beginnings of a way of conceptualizing how classes, constituted at the fundamental level of production relations, come to provide the basis of the social authority, the political sway and cultural domination of a 'class alliance on behalf of capital', without reducing the idea to what Marx once called the 'dirty-jewish' question of class interest, narrowly conceived. This latter form of economic reductionism, Gramsci argues, conceives of history as 'a continuous *marche de dupes*, a competition in conjuring and sleight of hand. "Critical" activity [i.e. Marxism] is reduced to the exposure of swindles, to creating scandals, and to prying into the pockets of public figures' (*Prison Notebooks*, ibid.). Which of us cannot quickly recall *that* brand of Marxism of exposure?

Gramsci's third contribution in this area is the attention he paid to the nature, specifically, of the *capitalist* state, its role in the generation of ideological consent, and thus to how class power secured itself in its 'decisive passage from the structure to the sphere of the complex superstructures', whilst at the same time providing, at the level of the superstructures and of ideologies, that 'cement' which welded the social formation together under the hegemonic sway of an alliance founded on the fundamental class of capital. 'In reality, the State must be conceived of as an "educator", in as much as it tends precisely to create a new type or level of civilization. Because one is acting essentially on economic forces reorganizing and developing the apparatus of economic production, creating a new structure, the conclusion must not be drawn that the superstructural factors should be left to themselves to develop spontaneously, to a haphazard and sporadic germination. The State, in this field too, is an instrument of rationalization, of acceleration and of Taylorization. It operates according to a plan, urges, incites, solicits, "punishes"; for once the conditions are created in which a certain way of life is "possible", then criminal action or omission must have a punitive sanction, with moral implications, and not merely be judged generically as "dangerous". The Law is the repressive and negative aspect of the entire, positive, civilizing activity undertaken by the State.'

A Marxist grasp of the nature of the State and its functions and processes under capitalism, especially in its classical 'liberal' or laissez-faire form, and the complementary discussion of 'consent' and 'coercion', of the role of ideology and common sense, etc., which fill out Gramsci's subtle and perceptive thought on this question, has rarely if ever been surpassed. Gramsci's work remains, of course, theoretically underdeveloped: the concepts are often in what Althussereans would call their 'practical' state: they are hardly ever 'pure' – never thoroughly or radically dismembered from their location within specific conjunctures. But if Lenin was correct to argue that what a Marxist analysis pointed to as its proper conclusion was the 'concrete analysis of a concrete situation' – in other words, precisely, the analysis of conjunctures – then it is Lenin himself, first, and Gramsci immediately behind who – in so far as such an analysis embraces the superstructures – lead the way.

Gramsci is the one 'Historicist' whose work continues to haunt, and can never be expunged from the starting points which the structuralists, like Althusser and Poulantzas, the other major contributors to a Marxist theory of base and superstructure, adopt. Both Althusser and Poulantzas criticize Gramsci's starting position within a 'philosophy of praxis' (cf. 'Marxism Is Not a Historicism', Althusser, *Reading Capital*, 1971; 'The Capitalist State And Ideologies', in Poulantzas, *Political Power and Social Classes*, 1973). Both are *massively* indebted to Gramsci, in seminal not just in marginal or incidental ways. Poulantzas's work on the political instance and on the State is conceptually impossible without Gramsci. And, as Althusser has revised his more 'theoreticist' earlier positions and moved towards a more substantive, less epistemological approach to the object of Marxist analysis (as for example in his seminal and extremely influential essay, 'Ideology and the State' in *Lenin and Philosophy, and Other Essays*, 1971) so his debt to Gramsci, already handsomely acknowledged, becomes both more explicit and more pronounced. The concept of 'ideological State apparatus', which has become a generative idea in the post-Althusserean analysis of the capitalist State, is a direct reworking of a few seminal passages on apparatuses of consent and coercion in Gramsci's 'State And Civil Society' essay (*Prison Notebooks*); though, of course, translated – with effect – into a more structuralist Marxist language.

Althusser

The contribution of Althusser and his followers, especially Poulantzas, in elaborating a Marxist theory of base/superstructure, is too complicated a matter to undertake here. We can only note three significant aspects which, taking up in his customarily rigorous fashion, Althusser has deeply transformed; thereby making a contribution of considerable theoretical significance to the problem of base and superstructure.

First, let us note that, in the manner in which a social formation is 'thought' by Althusser – beginning with the formative and classic essay, 'Contradiction and Over-determination', in *For Marx*, and developed in *Reading Capital* – there is more than a hint that the topographical metaphor of 'base/superstructure' ought to be superseded altogether. For Althusser conceives a social formation as composed of different *practices* – essentially the economic, political and ideological (with, perhaps, a fourth: theoretical practice?) – each of which is required for the production and reproduction of the relations of the capitalist mode: and each of which has its own inner constitution, its own specificity, its own dynamic and 'relative autonomy' from the others. Some of Althusser's most effective polemical passages are indeed reserved for taking the base/superstructure metaphor *literally*: and thus showing the absurdity of waiting for a historical moment when the determining level – His Majesty, the Economy – could detach itself from its more incidental and epiphenomenal superstructural forms, and exert its 'determination' over a social formation on its own! Neither in time nor history can 'determination in the last instance by the economic' be so read as to suggest that the level of economic practice could stand free and appear denuded of political and ideological practices.

This theory of the necessity, as well as of the 'relative autonomy', of the practices formerly consigned to the 'superstructures' – as we have already seen – constitutes one end of the double chain of a Marxist theory of a social formation. But then, what of the other end of the chain? How, then, is determinacy to be understood?

It is not, in Althusser's view, to be understood in terms of what produces a particular conjuncture, especially a revolutionary conjuncture. Such moments of fundamental rupture are no more exclusively produced by the single determinacy of 'the economic' than any other moment. Such moments are constituted, rather, by the accumulation of the different contradictions, peculiar to each of the levels or practices, in one space or moment: hence, such conjunctures are, like Freud's symptoms (from whom, indeed, the metaphor is adopted), not determined, but *'over*-determined'. Determinacy, then, for Althusser, is thought principally in terms of the economic level (determining) having, as one of its effects, the deciding which of the levels of the social formation – economic, political or ideological – will be 'dominant'.

Each level or practice is, thus, conceived, not as autonomous but as part of a 'complex, structured whole, structured in dominance'. Determinacy consists in the combination or articulation (the *Darstellung*) of instances and effects in and through this complex structure. 'The fact that each of these times and each of these histories is relatively autonomous does not make them so many domains which are independent of the whole; the specificity of each of these times and each of these histories – in other words, their relative autonomy and independence – is based on a certain type of dependence with respect to the whole' (*Reading Capital*). This is a conception of 'determination' rigorously reinterpreted in the form of what Althusser calls a 'structural' rather than a sequential causality. The whole point of *Reading Capital* is indeed to establish, via a 'symptomatic reading' of Marx's work, that this is indeed the form of 'causality' which the mature Marx employed.

The theoreticism, the 'straightening out' of Marx in the interests of proving his structuralist lineage, which is characteristic especially of Althusser's work in the period of *Reading Capital*, has been widely criticized; not least by some of his former collaborators (e.g. Rancière), and by Althusser himself (Althusser, 1976). But this should not detract from the seminal advance which the base-superstructure problem has undergone in his hands. This is brought forcefully forwards in the now-famous 'Ideological State Apparatuses' essay, in which Althusser puts forwards some Notes on the nature of ideology and the State, and restores some of the problems he had previously addressed to the more classical terrain of the 'class struggle' (actually, both here and in Poulantzas, more often invoked than present, as a concept performing the work of knowledge, in their respective texts). Again, the 'ISA's' essay cannot be resumed here. It requires careful and critical reading. It falls very much into two parts; and the first – which examines the locating of ideology in the apparatuses and structures of the State – is far more convincing than the second, which, following the sinuous path of a Lacanian revision of Freud, enters, it seems to us, another problematic which, however important, is as yet hardly within hailing distance of any which can be attributed to Marx without straining credibility.

What is most significant from our point of view here, however, is the manner in which the 'effectivity' of the superstructures is posed in this essay. Althusser recapitulates the central position in Marxism occupied by the base/superstructure metaphor. It is, he suggests, a metaphor: a 'metaphor of topography'. It 'makes something visible' – namely 'that the upper floors could not "stay up" alone, if they did not rest precisely on their base'. Despite Althusser's probing irony here at the expense of this topographical depiction, he acknowledges that it has a function: 'the great theoretical advantage of the Marxist topography . . . is simultaneously that it reveals that questions of determination (or of index of effectivity) are crucial: that it reveals that it is the base which in the last instance determines the whole edifice; and that, as a consequence, it obliges us to pose the theoretical problem of the type of "derivatory" effectivity peculiar to the superstructure, i.e. it obliges us to think what the Marxist tradition calls conjointly the relative autonomy of the superstructures and the reciprocal action of the superstructure on the base.' Thus, while retaining the classical metaphor, Althusser proposes to go beyond its purely descriptive limitations, and rethink the problem 'on the basis of reproduction'. What he means, broadly, by this is that the specific 'effectivity' of the superstructures is to be understood in terms of their role in *the reproduction of the social relations of production*; or what has come to be terms, on the basis of the problematic of 'social reproduction'.

Althusser makes, at best, a tentative start in this essay with this concept. The idea of regarding the superstructures in terms of social reproduction has, however, already proved innovative and productive conceptually, not least in those areas of Marxist theory (for example, in relation to the family, the sexual division of labour and the role of so-called 'unproductive labour') which have hitherto hardly survived the reductive thrust of the originating topographical metaphor. It is true that the notion of 'social reproduction' tends to produce in its wake its own distortion: that of an endlessly successful, functionally unfolding, reproduction of capitalist social relations without either end, contradiction, crisis or break. But then, the one question which Althussereans, in their peremptory haste to dismantle empirical and historicist-humanism forever ('Marxism is not a Humanism', 'Marxism is not Historicism'), have not deeply enough considered is whether, in declaring that Marxism is a 'structuralism' they have sufficiently satisfied themselves – or us – that Marxism is *not a functionalism*. However, while bearing this crucial but difficult theoretical issue in view, it must be said that the attempt to reconceptualize the base/superstructure problem in terms of 'social reproduction', and thus in much closer conceptual touch with the starting point of Marx's mature work (production, reproduction), has done a great deal to revivify theoretical work on the problem, and to set work on it moving in what may well prove to be a fruitful direction.

To take this conceptual opening further – both to modify and to extend it, critically – is, at the same time, to advance Marxism as a critical science and as a theoretically informed revolutionary practice. Only when we can grasp and comprehend the dense, opaque integument of capitalist societies – their base and their complex superstructures – through the former are we likely to be able to develop a sufficiently informed practice to transform them.

LIST OF REFERENCES

Althusser, 1968: *For Marx*, Allen Lane, Penguin Press.

Anderson, 1976: *Considerations on Western Marxism*, New Left Books.

Callinicos, 1976: *Althusser's Marxism*, Pluto Press.

Geras, 1972: 'Marx and the Critique of Political Economy', in R. Blackburn (ed.), *Ideology in Social Science*, Fontana.

Geras, 1971: 'Fetishism in Marx's *Capital*', in *New Left Review* 65.

Glucksmann, 1972: 'The Althusserian Theatre', in *New Left Review* 72.

Hall, 1974: 'Marx's Notes on Method: A Reading of the 1857 *Introduction*', in *Working Papers in Cultural Studies*, in *WPCS 6*, Centre for Contemporary Cultural Studies, Birmingham.

Marx, 1961: *Capital*, vol. 1, Foreign Languages Publishing House, Moscow.

Marx, 1971: *A Contribution to the Critique of Political Economy*, Lawrence and Wishart.

Marx, 1973: *Surveys from Exile*, D. Fernbach (ed.), Penguin/*New Left Review*, Harmondsworth.

MESW, 1951: Marx/Engels, Selected Works. Lawrence and Wishart.

Mepham, 1974: 'The Theory of Ideology in *Capital*', in *WPCS 6*, Centre for Contemporary Cultural Studies, Birmingham.

Poulantzas, 1973: *Political Power and Social Classes*, New Left Books/Sheed and Ward.

BOURGEOIS HEGEMONY IN VICTORIAN BRITAIN

ROBERT GRAY

This paper analyses the relationships between the economically dominant bourgeoisie, ideology and the state during the nineteenth century, in terms of the concepts of hegemony and the power bloc, formulated by Gramsci and developed by Poulantzas.[1] The location of political hegemony in this formation was among the issues debated by Perry Anderson and E. P. Thompson, and clarified in an illuminating comment by Poulantzas.[2] In this paper I follow Thompson and Poulantzas in locating hegemony in the bourgeoisie, and amplify this thesis in a discussion of the nature of the Victorian ruling class, relations among its fractions, and the 'hegemonizing' practices through which consent was organized, both among the allied fractions constituting the dominant power bloc and in their relations to the classes they ruled.

One major theoretical difficulty should be noted at the outset. It is extremely difficult to avoid formulations that suggest a conspiratorial and mechanistic view of the class struggle. This reflects limitations to the concepts and language available to a British Marxist historian in the 1970s. Thus it is now widely recognized as a general principle that Marxism is not a 'conspiracy thesis', that politics and ideology cannot be reduced to mere instruments of the subjective will of the dominant class, and that classes are not heavenly hosts to be 'marshalled, sent on manœuvres, and marched up and down whole centuries'.[3] But it is not easy to move from these general caveats to specific analyses without adopting formulations that personify classes; the implicit model of class struggle is a boxing match or a game of chess between two rival class-subjects. I certainly would not claim to resolve this problem; we probably lack the concepts and language to do so. But I do want to suggest that Gramsci provides an indispensable point of approach. The necessary theoretical advances will come from deploying the resources he provides in concrete historical research, with a conscious effort to purge conspiratorial and mechanistic formulations from the vocabulary of Marxist analysis.

Characteristics of the Victorian bourgeoisie

Nineteenth-century capitalism was competitive capitalism, and this has important implications for the nature of its ruling class.[4] Industrial, commercial and banking capital were separately owned, in contrast to their merger into finance capital during the twentieth-century monopoly era; and each fraction was itself composed of many competing rival capitals, as yet little affected by concentration and centralization. Big landowners still constituted either a separate class or a very distinctive fraction.

The competitive industrial capitalism of the period was, moreover, one of family businesses and private partnerships, with a localized basis (decreasingly so from the 1880s, but still significantly so – especially as compared to the more newly industrialized countries of Germany and the USA – down to 1914). Even quite big industrialists had strong local roots in the factory towns of the North and Midlands. Banking capital, on the other hand, was probably growing in importance, as overseas investment grew, and gathered around itself a 'rentier' bourgeoisie. Concentrated especially in London and the southern counties (and in Scotland in Edinburgh), this fraction diverged in attitudes and probably at times in interests from industrial capital. It had close links with the central State apparatus (located of course in the capital city), perhaps because direct day-to-day influence on government was vital to its interests (e.g. imperialist intervention in support of bondholders).

This schematic characterization of the Victorian ruling class breaks with the conventional wisdom of contemporaries, and many historians, who saw society as divided into an 'aristocracy', 'middle classes' and 'working classes'. The 'middle classes' embraced both sections of the dominant bourgeoisie and sections of the 'middle strata' (shopkeepers, tradesmen, many professional practitioners, white-collar employees, etc.). The prevalence of this notion is a measure of the success with which such strata were subordinated to bourgeois hegemony – to the point where the real differences in class position were obscured – but also a measure of the economic realities which made this possible: the predominance of local-based businesses, whose owners were not too remote from a broader base of medium and small 'petty bourgeois' businessmen. This means that to identify members of the ruling class is often a complicated matter, demanding close analysis of a range of sources for the local formation under study.[5] There was also doubtless a good deal of individual movement between the top layers of the middle strata and the fringes of the ruling class. The distinction between the class positions of these groups is nonetheless a real one, whatever the limitations of our information about particular cases (an empirical difficulty which cannot be allowed to dictate the conceptual framework we adopt).

The relationship of the bourgeoisie to the landowners (I say 'landowners' as a deliberately neutral descriptive term) also poses problems. To what extent can the landowners (whose position rested on the success of capitalist agriculture conducted by their tenant farmers, but increasingly also on other forms of investment) be seen as a separate class, as opposed to a fraction of the bourgeoisie? How real was their apparent antagonism to the urban-industrial bourgeoisie in the first half of the nineteenth century? Does their dominance over key sectors of the state and their indisputable wealth, social prestige and influence mean that they, rather than the owners of industrial capital, were the hegemonic fraction of the ruling class? The class determination of the landowners can perhaps be treated as an open question for the purposes of the present discussion (I would, however, incline to the view of Thompson and Poulantzas that they constitute a fraction of capital rather than a separate class);[6] what is important is to recognize their existence as a highly distinctive group, whose interests were strongly articulated and whose culture and values were in important respects different from those of the urban ruling class.

Finally, we must note the particular position and role of the ruling class intellectuals, those groups to be found exercising leadership at the head of the State apparatus and in the elaboration and reproduction of dominant ideology. The term 'urban gentry' has been aptly applied to these groups.[7] Particularly concerned with the administrative and ideological organization of society, they were to be found as members of statistical societies and Royal Commissions, writers and readers of the quarterly press, organizers of charity and social discipline. Drawn from the professions (though by no means every professional man could be placed in the category), from intellectually gifted protégés of the wealthy, or from established wealth whose owners could devote time (like Charles Booth) to 'social problems', they played a crucial role in the organization of hegemony. Their social affinities and attitudes varied in ways which show a complex correspondence to the different bourgeois fractions; but they also, as is characteristic of intellectuals, had particular 'caste-like' modes of cohesion, and links with socially broader based intellectual strata;[8] the definition of 'genteel' professional status and qualifications, and the associated transformation and growth of high prestige educational institutions, were important developments of the period, forming hierarchies of intellectuals, but at the same time fostering their cohesion on a 'professional' basis.

The power bloc

Most historians would agree that the late 1840s and early 50s saw an important shift in the economic, political and ideological relations in British society. The various accounts of this process have in common an emphasis on the establishment of stable relations of political and ideological domination in an industrial-urban society. This historically unprecedented transition was rendered more problematic by the fact that Britain was the first industrial nation; but this same peculiarity gave certain historic advantages to British capital. The early bourgeois revolution, and subsequent development of the State and relations of hegemony, limited the challenges to capitalism. The emerging working-class political tradition had a dynamic sense of class identity and interest, and a developing concern to theorize the experience of class exploitation; yet the early forms of socialism never displaced the dominance of a radical-democratic tradition.

The stabilization and diversification of the economy in the years after 1850 was an important precondition for political stabilization. But the crisis was clearly not 'purely economic' (no historical phenomenon ever is) and stabilization had political and ideological dimensions that were not just mechanical reflections of the economic shift.[9] Stable class rule depended on the construction of a power bloc of allied dominant classes and fractions. In periods of 'organic crisis' the power bloc becomes unworkable (e.g. because it fails to represent newly important fractions of the bourgeoisie, such as industrial capital in the early nineteenth century, to mobilize the consent of new classes and strata, etc.) and tends to disintegrate;[10] the social instability of the second quarter of the century represents just such a crisis. In the power bloc constructed in the period of stabilization, landowners continued (despite the sharp antagonisms of the preceding decades, in whose diminution the solidarity of the 'propertied classes' against the Chartist threat had played a large part) to dominate important sectors of the State, 'as the *aristocratic representatives* of the bourgeoisie, of the industrial and commercial middle class'.[11]

State power thus presents the appearance of a kind of equilibrium. In the 1830s the new urban areas had gained parliamentary representation and the right to constitute ratepayer-controlled municipal corporations, to establish police forces controlled by watch committees, etc. Politics in such areas contained some popular elements, generally channelled by groups and parties representing the local bourgeoisie. (Local government was often the preserve of shopkeepers and tradesmen, who manifested a certain antagonism to the local ruling class, but were unable to use their electoral power to strike at its position.)[12] Rural areas were still administered by gentry sitting on the magistrates' bench, and parliamentary representation was normally in the gift of the biggest of these landowners; politics there was not unlike what it had been in the eighteenth century. The landowners were strongly represented in party leadership and cabinets, whose formal political complexion was a range of loose and shifting Whig–Liberal and Liberal–Whig coalitions, until the extension of the urban vote in 1867 led to a more clear-cut party system adapted to mass urban politics. 'Territorial influence', 'virtual representation' and 'a stake in the community' were pervasive political concepts. Put together, they amounted to the notion that the leading property-holders (whether gentry or merchants and industrialists) were the natural representatives of their communities, and that the political participation of other groups should be dependent on a properly rational social demeanour, as defined by their superiors (a notion modified, but not entirely overthrown, by the extension of the vote in 1867 to many urban workers, who were held to have a kind of corporate stake by virtue of saving in friendly societies, co-ops, etc.).[13]

Hegemony in the power bloc

The effect of this political configuration was to reproduce capitalist relations, and to foster especially the expansion of industrial capital. The industrial bourgeoisie constituted the *hegemonic fraction* within the power bloc – that whose interests preponderate in the exercise of state power, and whose particular social relations figure in dominant ideological representations. This hegemonic position is not synonomous with the *governing fraction* (in this period partly landowners) which staffs the top levels of the State apparatus, or the groups which elaborate and reproduce dominant ideology (the leading intellectuals: in this case the 'urban gentry').[14] Hegemony should not be located in those groups which visibly exercise political and ideological leadership in society, but rather in the *effects* of dominant forms of political and ideological practice, the particular social relations they reproduce. The location of hegemony is historically problematic and may show complex shifts and displacements within the dominant class and its forms of political representation.

It is therefore necessary to look in more detail at the ways in which the industrial bourgeoisie exerted hegemony over the power bloc and the State apparatus. Two important aspects of this should be mentioned. First, the pervasive power of bourgeois ideas about economic life and the absence of theoretically articulated alternatives. Various overlapping intellectual and literary networks produced administrative cadres strongly committed to utilitarianism and free trade, who staffed key new branches of the State apparatus.[15] Moreover 'divinity and economics ran together'[16] and the laws of political economy were closely entangled with moral, and often religiously sanctioned, norms of 'rational conduct'. The secularized prescriptions of utility and economic progress and the strong religious components of hegemonic ideology in practice reinformed each other; the utilitarians offered the only available techniques for dealing with the 'merely *business* side of the social arrangements'.[17] A new notion of 'public opinion' – the influence of the élite press, the legitimizing functions of professional expertise, the political technique of the Royal Commission, whose proceedings could be stagemanaged and anyhow reflected unspoken shared assumptions – developed with the activities of utilitarian and Evangelical pressure-groups.

The terrain of the State and of public discussion and policy-making was thus re-shaped by the intellectuals of the industrial bourgeoisie;[18] the landowners, as the Whigs realized in 1832 and as Peel realized in the 1840s, had to adapt to this terrain. Their adaptation occurred at many levels, from the supremacy of vulgarized political economy and of the national goal of industrial progress, to the 'reform of manners' noted by many contemporaries and historians. While it is doubtful if 'Victorian middle-class' norms of conduct ever really captured the hearts of the landowners (or even of the urban bourgeoisie themselves) as a whole, there was a significant measure of external conformity to norms of domestic life and sexual morality, religious observance, and serious application to public service as the obligation of social privilege.

Secondly, the local character of much State power – including such key coercive organs as the police and the poor law – and the correspondingly local 'provincial' basis of industry make the composition of the central State apparatus a misleading guide; with the limited role of the State, 'hegemony over its historical development belongs to private forces, to civil society – which is "State" too',[19] and among these 'private forces' industrial capital dominated in the expanding urban areas. The power bloc of the third quarter of the nineteenth century rested on the local predominance of industrialists, merchants and bourgeois intellectuals in the towns, together with a measure of direct urban bourgeois representation in parliament and key branches of civil service, and ideological hegemony cemented by the institutions of 'informed public opinion'. The role of landowners in government and the state has to be set firmly in this context; 'let them govern, but let them be fit to govern',[20] as one industrialist put it, summing up in ten words the relation between hegemonic and governing fractions.

The power bloc should not be seen as monolithic. In every social formation the State apparatus has important internal contradictions, but also specific modes of cohesion as an apparatus. 'This unity . . . is not established in a simple fashion, either by some kind of united act of will . . . , or because the . . . [hegemonic fraction] have got a physical stranglehold on the state-instrument as a whole. . . . It is rather established in a complex fashion, depending on the class contradiction, by means of a whole chain involving the subordination of certain apparatuses to others which particularly condense the power of the hegemonic fraction; involving under-determinations, short-circuits and doublings-up between real power and formal power; shifts of apparatuses from the ideological field to the field of the repressive apparatus and vice versa; finally, significant changes within each apparatus itself.'[21]

A study of the Victorian civil service appears to exemplify the processes of 'subordination of certain apparatuses to others', shifts in functions and prestige, and so on. The effect of the activity of bourgeois utilitarian intellectual cadres was to bring about such re-organizations and shifts, and thereby to 'condense the power of the hegemonic fraction'. Thus different branches of the State apparatus (e.g. different civil service departments) had different traditions, modes of recruitment, social affinities, styles of work, etc.[22] Those established in the eighteenth century or before (army, foreign office, home office) were particularly likely to be repositories of 'aristocratic' values and styles, and to provoke the wrath of the more radical bourgeois reformers; while new branches established in the nineteenth century (including those dealing with distinctively 'nineteenth century' problems of economic and social policy: e.g. the Board of Trade, Local Government Board, Education Department, etc.) conformed more closely to utilitarian models of a public bureaucracy. (This should not, however, be taken to imply some kind of 'meritocratic' career structure; the concern of reformers was much more with how civil servants acted than with broadening their social composition, and criteria of professional competence if anything increased the importance of an educational level attainable only at a limited range of institutions.) To establish the location of hegemony thus demands a close study of differences within the state apparatus and of relations between its branches. Such a study does not sustain Perry Anderson's thesis of a 'symbiotic fusion' of bourgeoisie and aristocracy, in which the bourgeoisie abandoned any claim to ideological hegemony; the features he notices – utilitarian empiricism, indifference to any global theory of society, the mystique of 'tradition' and the dominance of a narrowly commonsensical practicality – may rather be interpreted as measures of the depth and strength of the hegemony of industrial capital.[23]

Political parties (understood in a broad sense of the term) played a crucial part in hegemony over the State apparatus. The construction of viable power blocs does not emanate from a far-sighted plan elaborated by some secret committee of the dominant class; it is the effect of struggles between parties, which always represent *combinations* of classes and fractions (including some measure of representation of dominated classes and strata).[24] Its existence can never be taken for granted, as a datum of political life, but is reproduced through political struggle in every historical conjuncture. It is for this reason that it is in my view mystifying to write in ways that impute to classes and fractions a kind of individual subjectivity, as though they took decisions, adopted stategies, formed alliances, and so on in a unitary and un-problematic fashion; in effect, this treats parties – and hence the whole political and ideological level – as epiphenomenal, whereas in reality classes are constituted by class struggle, which always involves their representation in parties.[25] And party cleavages – whether within the power bloc or in the social formation as a whole – do not reflect class differences in a simple reductive fashion; parties are efficacious in so far as they have *some* support in *all* classes and fractions, and cohere partly through specifically ideological (in the nineteenth century often religious) differences and traditions.

The term 'party' is here used in the broad sense of Gramsci, not in the more restricted sense of the formal party system. It is perhaps particularly those institutions and practices held to be 'outside politics', to stand above the struggle of formal parties (which are confined to the representative parts of the state) that condense the power of the hegemonic fraction. The State itself, Gramsci suggests, cements the power bloc under the hegemony of a particular class or fraction, and in this sense acts as a 'party' organizing the dominant class.[26] The ideology of the bourgeois intellectuals was characterized by a disdain for the rough and tumble of party politics, and a belief that sound administration and public service (based of course on a sound know-ledge of the indisputable 'laws' of political economy) stood 'above politics'; they thus constituted 'an élite of men of culture, who have the function of providing leadership of a cultural and general ideological nature for a great movement of interrelated parties (which in reality are fractions of one and the same organic party)'.[27]

To see formal party differences as 'in reality fractions of one and the same organic party' is in no sense to reduce their importance. Hegemonic ideology had differentiated versions and interpretations, and was constantly argued out and re-formulated within the ruling class. The debate about factory legislation, for example, was at this level a debate around the bourgeois value of the integrity of the family, which was held to be threatened by the employment of women and children, and thus came into contradiction with the ideology of freedom of contract, including freedom to buy and sell female and child labour. A whole series of debates about the proper limits of public regulation – sanitation, housing, education, etc. – can be viewed in similar terms. There might also be divergences of a 'strategic' or 'tactical' nature (that is to say, differences of opinion which appeared ideologically as differences about the best course to ensure the preservation of a given social group). Thus the party conflict between Whig and Tory landowners in 1832 was partly about whether it was better to make concessions to the urban 'middle classes' and thus gain their support for 'the constitution', or whether any concession was dangerous; and the Tory party split on similar lines over the corn laws in 1846.

The power bloc should therefore not be seen as static, but as constantly re-constituted, modified, strengthened or undermined in party struggles. There were two main possibilities of mobilizing political support during the period after 1850, corresponding roughly to 'urban' (Liberal) and 'rural' (Tory) political formations. But there was significant urban, and even radical working class, support for the Tories, and Liberals often sought to weaken the landowners by claiming to represent the interests of farmers and farm labourers, thus splitting the rural bloc. The Whigs, as a party of big landowners in uneasy and shifting alliance with urban Liberalism, occupied a commanding but somewhat ambiguous political position. All parliamentary majorities had to be composed of some elements from both the 'urban' and 'rural' camps. Nevertheless the difference between 'urban'/Liberal and 'rural'/Tory constituted the main line of political cleavage in the decades after 1850, until the changes of the 1880s and 90s once more threw party alignments into the melting-pot. It was the 'formula' on which politics was conducted, and alliances cutting across this formula did not have the effect of disintegrating the two main socio-political blocs; Peel, for example, failed to make the Tories the party of an alliance between the landed interest and the urban 'middle classes', partly because of back-bench opposition in 1846 which found a leader in Disraeli.

The power bloc was therefore the result of party struggles, in which real antagonisms were at stake. The areas of 'aristocratic' domination were often challenged by political leaders claiming to speak for the dynamic urban society of free competition and industrial progress against hereditary privilege, patronage and corruption. Marx, perhaps with the idea that the historic mission of the bourgeoisie was to make a revolution on the French model lurking at the back of his mind, expected such antagonisms to be fought through to a conclusion, and thus greatly under-estimated the solidity and permanency of the power bloc whose lineaments he correctly discerned.[28] For there can be no doubt that the continuing 'aristocratic' presence had objective advantages for the urban bourgeoisie. Bagehot's analysis of mass deference and the 'dignified part of the constitution' is often correctly cited in this context.[29] But its significance did not lie merely in the 'deferential' support it attracted, but equally in the opposition it provoked from the radical workers and petty bourgeoisie, whose demagogic leadership by bourgeois politicians (the Anti-Corn Law League in the 1840s, the agitation for parliamentary reform in the 60s, Joseph Chamberlain in the 80s) helped cement Liberal hegemony over mass popular radicalism.[30]

Two political alliances were thus possible for parties of the urban bourgeoisie: a 'conservative' (in the general, rather than party, sense of the term) bloc of big urban and rural property, relying for its mass base on the 'territorial influence' of the landowners (in party terms: Tories + Whigs + some Liberals); or a radical-liberal bloc of urban classes and strata, finding its ideological cohesion in hostility to the 'aristocracy' (in party terms: Radicals + Liberals + some Whigs). The power bloc which existed corresponded to neither of these models: but it was the effect of party struggles, which tended to polarize along the axis of these alternatives, and to move towards one or other pole with each new conjuncture of class forces.

Hegemony and the subordinate classes

The period after *c.* 1850 is generally seen as one during which the working class became less combative and less united, beginning to pursue limited interests within a society whose general framework was rarely questioned. This consent to capitalist relations was organized through a complex set of processes, which certainly cannot be reduced, as vulgarizations of the concept of hegemony would have it, to some notion of 'social control', or the unilateral imposition 'from above' of ideological uniformity. To talk of the 'organization of consent' implies a political practice ('hegemonization') through which diverse, and often potentially 'subversive', ideological practices are subordinated and contained. Conversely, the adoption 'for reasons of submission and intellectual subordination'[31] of a language drawn from the ideological practice of the dominant class always implies a shift in the meanings of that language. Ideology is the 'lived relation between men and their world',[32] and in a differentiated social formation can never be uniform. Hence there are contradictions within the practices which maintain the hegemony of the dominant class, and this hegemony should be seen as a dynamic and historically shifting set of relations, not as a static system of manipulative control.

Nor should we oversimplify the distinction between 'coercion' and 'consent'. As Gramsci himself emphasized, any form of hegemony presupposes particular relations of coercion, and vice versa; effective domination depends on a workable combination of 'voluntary' and 'coercive' relations.[33] One feature of the containment of working-class opposition in the 1830s and 40s was the extremely discriminating use of legal repression, often with considerable care to ensure the prior political isolation of its victims. Coercion itself may, moreover, have symbolic aspects, as the rituals of legal repression testify. No set of relations is ever 'purely' coercive, since all systems of coercion require at the very least effective hegemony over the personnel of the coercive organs themselves; the organization of consent is a precondition of stable rule even in fascist dictatorships.[34] My emphasis on hegemony should not therefore be taken to imply the absence of force; indeed the growth of the state apparatus, including new repressive organs such as the police, was a feature of the period, which its liberal rhetoric should not be permitted to obscure.

Hegemony, then, should not be seen as reproduced solely through institutions of a self-evidently 'political' or 'ideological' character; the political and ideological are present in *all* social relations.[35] Thus the most important aspect of hegemony over the working class (both in the nineteenth and twentieth centuries) is their forced habituation to the relations of industrial wage-labour, and the ideological practices involved in this process; the cycle of capitalist production reproduces the capitalist as capitalist and the wage-labourer as wage-labourer at the ideological, as well as economic, level. One aspect of the explosive class struggles before 1850 was the newness of factory employment, and the struggle to resist the real subordination of wage-labour to capital in the process of production itself, as opposed to the merely 'formal' subordination characteristic of domestic industry.[36] In the 1850s the new mode of production was more firmly established; the possibility of transforming it seemed remote, and economic diversification and stabilization meant that visible advances, albeit of a highly sectional character, could be won by bargaining within the system. Capitalist production was a relatively fixed environment, to which all sections of the working class had, in varying ways, to adapt. And this adaptation, the necessary condition of individual survival, extended to areas of life-style, personal conduct, even in some cases religious belief and observance. The enormous relative strength of Victorian employers (even in trades with 'strong' craft unions by the standards of the time, still more so in unorganized sectors) accentuated the inherent despotism of industrial capital.

But it was not only at work that the bourgeoisie sought to produce an ideological environment to which workers had to adapt. One response to the social crisis of the 1830s and 40s was an 'evangelistic' (in both a specifically religious and general metaphorical sense of the term) drive to assert control over the urban masses. This is especially clear in the concern with education, whose ideological assumptions were stated with an explicitness that seems remarkable to anyone accustomed to the more veiled terms of such discussions nowadays (this 'frankness' is presumably related to the self-confidence of the bourgeoisie at a period when capitalism could be seen as synonymous with economic progress).[37] Social unrest was seen as the result of indiscipline, the lack of moral control by social superiors, and 'ignorance'. Remedies were believed to include poor law reform, the beginnings of elementary education, religious evangelism, propaganda against dangerous 'economic heresies', the fostering of more acceptable expressions of working-class self help (friendly societies, co-ops, etc.) and of safe forms of 'rational recreation'.

In all these activities the urban gentry were very much to the fore. Common to all of them was the attempt to propagate an ideology common to the ruling class as a whole, but also with certain traits specific to the urban gentry.[38] Economic, moral and religious concerns were fused into a single image of urban social danger; iron laws, whether of calvinist theology or classical economics, dictated discipline and restraint, the slightest backsliding would lead to disaster, and individual weakness could spread contagiously to demoralize society and reverse the precarious conquest of scarcity achieved through industriousness and foresight. To convince the working class of the truth of this, through varying forms of persuasion and coercion, was the common theme of a range of bourgeois endeavours in the urban community. The urban gentry were distinguished by the rigour with which they elaborated this outlook (e.g. they agitated against dilutions of the 1834 poor law, while other bourgeois groups adopted a more pragmatic attitude). The second distinctive feature is a paternalistic colouring, the attempt to reproduce in urban society the harmonious social hierarchy supposed, in a highly ideological view of social conflict, to characterize a lost rural world. Both features reflect their social location as bourgeois intellectuals, distanced from the realities of industrial production. Hence, perhaps, the centrality of the family, where ideologies of subordination and control (over women, children and servants) could be acted out, as they could not in the world of industrial production.[39] Conversely, the moral decay of the working class was seen above all in terms of its deficient patterns of family life, the apparent absence of values of domesticity, family responsibility, thrift and accumulation. The concern with the urban environment reflected a preoccupation, not with bad conditions as such, but with their disintegrating effect on family relations (as, for example, in the 1884 Royal Commission on Housing where incest in overcrowded dwellings is a recurring preoccupation).

The urban gentry sought, then, to resolve the problems of capitalist society by a network of direct or indirect controls designed to reform the individual behaviour of the working class. During the crisis of the 1830s and 40s this was pursued with an almost hysterical evangelism. Its success was limited until the crisis period ended, but from the 1850s changes in the working class (the emergence of the labour aristocracy) could be read as comforting signs of 'progress', and evangelical zeal was tempered by social complacency.

Does this evangelical re-structuring of the urban community represent the successful imposition of bourgeois values? It is often so treated. But to see it like that is to read contemporary statements at face value, and to reduce hegemony to the subjective intentions of members of the ruling class, or to a functionalist problematic of 'social control'. The most effective ideological influences came, not from the evangelical social reform that sought to eradicate working-class identity altogether, but from more complex and indirect agencies, through which fragments of dominant ideology were 'spontaneously' reproduced by members of the working class. Those programmes through which a group seeks to influence ways of thinking and acting are not necessarily the most adequate or effective forms of hegemony (though they may be extremely important to the cohesion and morale of the ruling class itself, as they were in this case): nor should behaviour that apparently corresponds to dominant ideology be read at face value as a direct product of ruling class influence.

Viable forms of hegemony had to take account of the situation and aspirations of the working class, especially of its organized and articulate sections: the labour aristocracy. Thus behaviour corresponding to such central values as 'thrift' and 'respectability' was certainly articulated and rationalized in the terms of dominant ideology, but it has still to be seen in relation to the distinctive social experience of different groups.[40] Thrift was linked to survival under the conditions of life confronting skilled labour; and self-help could take collective forms. Those labour aristocratic groups most likely to adopt such behaviour patterns were also most resistant to any form of patronage and direct control (indeed this independence was part of the meaning they attached to the values of 'respectability'). As the signs of a striving for 'respectability' among higher-paid workers were read as indicating social harmony and progress, so it became apparent that the distinctive identity of the working class could not simply be eradicated, but that the reproduction of dominant values rested on a more subtle process of negotiated re-definition, in which the conditional independence of working-class institutions came to be recognized. The ideological function of the law is apparent in discussions about such institutions as friendly societies and trade unions; the legal framework defined the boundaries of those forms of 'respectable' working-class behaviour considered legitimate.[41]

Because bourgeois hegemony involved negotiated re-definitions of values and the emergence of distinctive versions of the dominant ideology, and because that ideology could give no convincing account of aspects of real social experience, there were important tensions and contradictions in ideological relations between the classes. The independence of the labour aristocracy was only grudgingly and suspiciously accepted. Many institutions were rejected by their intended upper working-class clientèle because of their heavy management by patrons, as, for instance, were the mechanics' institutes; others, like the working men's clubs, had sharp internal struggles to throw off patronage.[42] Even those institutions that were strongly approved and assiduously fostered had a side the bourgeoisie found impenetrable, bewildering and disturbing (saving for funerals, ritual and conviviality in friendly societies). The extent to which working people could be trusted to run such institutions, and the terms on which they should be licensed to do so, is a main theme in official enquiries of the period.

Class tensions keep breaking through the rhetoric of 'respectability'. Class consciousness could be contained and eroded, but never eradicated. The high wages that underpinned the pursuit of 'respectability' depended on the organization and struggle of the craft unions. Trade unionism always drew a sharp line between the outlook of the labour aristocracy and that of their social superiors. Attempts by both sides to define 'acceptable' forms of trade unionism always proved exceedingly fragile.

Hegemony over the working class should therefore not be seen in terms of a re-moulding of the 'respectable' skilled strata in the bourgeois image. It arose from a complex set of social relations, in which bourgeois reform aimed at imposing social discipline was one, but only one, element. It would be equally true to say that relations of hegemony involved the imposition *on the bourgeoisie* of some form of representation, at all levels of social practice, of working-class interests (especially, but not exclusively, those of the labour aristocracy). When bourgeois intellectuals like Alfred Marshall praised the enlightened moderation of the 'largest and best managed unions'[43] this was something the bourgeoisie had been *forced* to accept, and to legitimize through shifts in its ideology, not a cunning scheme to 'integrate' the labour aristocracy. Any 'integration' was a two-edged affair, as the whole history of working-class struggle indicates.

The network of overlapping activities in the urban community which I have labelled 'bourgeois evangelism' was, however, significant for hegemony in two related ways. First, it fostered the cohesion and morale of the ruling class itself, provided a sense of mission, and a set of inter-related ideological accounts of the palpable social realities of Victorian capitalism. The norms of domestic life, religious observance, etc., helped draw ideological boundaries between those members of society able and willing to behave 'rationally', and the un-regenerate urban masses. (This does not mean, as is often implied, that any recognition of 'environmental' aspects of working-class behaviour was necessarily excluded by the dominant ideology; the point is that whether one started with the 'environment' or the 'individual' the analysis remained within the same given ideological assumptions.) Secondly, evangelistic reform played an important part in bourgeois hegemony over the middle strata, and especially in the production of 'subaltern intellectuals'.[44] The whole problem of hegemony over these groups has been veiled by the very strength of that hegemony.[45] Yet the small businessmen, white-collar employees, etc., had different relations of production from those of the bourgeoisie and inhabited a distinct social world, even though its upper fringes might overlap the world of the bourgeoisie.

Two features of dominant ideology seem important for hegemony over these strata: family and religion. Domestic life-style, often though not necessarily including the employment of domestic service, had an important symbolic function in defining membership of the 'middle class'; even for groups whose social relations were not those of capital, the pervasive metaphors of restraint, accumulation, and advance through the exercise of rational self-control could be applied to the visible status of the family. (These metaphors also, of course, could plausibly apply to the realities of incremental salaries, promotion, or the modest prosperity which the professional practitioner or small businessman saw as the reward of hard work.) Many churches, especially the English nonconformists and the Free Church of Scotland, drew their congregations from these strata. The greatest response to the urban missionary efforts seems to have come from the middle strata, rather than from the working class whose irreligion loomed so large in the social anxieties of some bourgeois intellectuals.

It was particularly from these sections of society that the 'subaltern intellectuals' of Victorian Britain were drawn – and also, in the case of intellectuals in the narrow professional sense (teachers, etc.), belonged by virtue of their occupational function. Elementary schoolteachers were recruited from the middle strata and upper layers of the working class; criteria of family respectability entered into their selection, and their relations with the school inspectors – at this period often urban gentry, who themselves had neither attended nor taught in elementary schools – symbolized their subordinate social role.[46] Other occupations have been less studied but are probably of equal significance in this respect; all the professions, for example, were heterogeneous in composition, divided between leading (bourgeois) and subaltern (middle strata) intellectuals. (The recruitment and function of the clergy might be especially interesting.) Other groups performed the social function of subaltern intellectuals without having the occupational status of an intellectual.[47] One effect of the party struggle was to form 'intellectuals' (in the broadest sense of the term) among the subordinate classes. The local political role of shopkeepers has already been mentioned; this role appears to have extended beyond the political sphere narrowly defined, to a range of institutions, with churches often forming vital links in the local institutional network.[48] The leaders of organized labour were another important grouping of intellectuals in the broad Gramscian sense; their significance certainly increased during the third quarter of the century, especially with the advent in the 1870s of working class representation in local and parliamentary government.

The period saw an expansion of such groups, which occupied a key position in the reproduction of relations of domination. But this should certainly not be interpreted in a mechanistic fashion; the subaltern intellectuals were more than mere 'transmission belts'. Their mode of life and, therefore, ideology were quite different from those of the bourgeoisie, and hegemony over them, and over the subordinate classes generally, depended on the representation within the hegemonic ideology of 'a number of "elements" which transcribe the way classes other than the hegemonic class live their conditions of existence'.[49] This is apparent in the relations between the bourgeoisie and the labour aristocracy, and the adaptations of bourgeois ideology to take account of the autonomous existence of working-class organizations. The same thing may hold for the middle strata, whose relations with the dominant class have been less well discussed by historians. Any electoral base in the towns depended on the mobilization of shop-keepers and tradesmen, and concessions (even if purely opportunistic concessions) to their outlook. And the proliferation of subaltern intellectuals led to modifications of the functions their social superiors had designed for them. 'Official' definitions of the scope and purposes of elementary education were, for example, modified in practice in the classroom – a process reinforced by the development of teachers' associations and after 1870 of elected School Boards. Religious institutions may also have undergone significant transformations, as evangelism found a response in the middle strata. Literary and scientific production by intellectuals from the subordinate classes might produce important innovations, to which the hegemonic ideology had to adapt.[50]

The role of the subaltern intellectuals was therefore two-sided. On one hand, they did transmit elements of ideology adopted 'from above'; but this was itself an active process, necessarily involving re-interpretation of ideological forms, their adaptation so as to render them 'plausible' under diverse social conditions. On the other hand, they also transmitted 'upwards' innovative ideological practices, which might be imposed on the hegemonic class itself. (Indeed the capacity to adapt to such innovations, and thus retain ideological leadership of a social bloc, is one measure of the strength of hegemony.) Hegemony was a set of political relations between classes, fractions and strata, and was fractured by contradictions. Historical shifts in the class struggle can only be understood in terms of this inherently contradictory character of relations of hegemony. The last two decades of the nineteenth century, for example, were characterized by social transformations which eroded the forms of domination examined in this paper, with consequent shifts and dislocations in the patterns of hegemony.

NOTES

1. A. Gramsci, *Prison Notebooks*, trans. and ed. Q. Hoare and G. Nowell Smith (1971); N. Poulantzas, *Classes in Contemporary Capitalism*, trans. D. Fernbach (1975). By 'hegemony' Gramsci meant those political practices through which consent to capitalist social relations is organized; the concept of 'power bloc', present in Gramsci but developed more explicitly by Poulantzas, refers to the fact that political power is generally exercised by an alliance of dominant classes and social groups.

2. P. Anderson, 'Origins of the Present Crisis', *New Left Review* 23 (1964); E. P. Thompson, 'The Peculiarities of the English', *Socialist Register 1965*, ed. R. Miliband and J. Saville; N. Poulantzas, 'Marxist Political Theory in Great Britain', *New Left Review* 43 (1967).

3. Thompson, op. cit., p. 357.

4. For general accounts of the period see especially: G. Best, *Mid-Victorian Britain* (original edn., 1971): M. Dobb, *Studies in the Development of Capitalism* (revised edn., 1963); E. J. Hobsbawm, *Industry and Empire* (1968) and *The Age of Capital* (1975).

5. J. Foster, *Class Struggle and the Industrial Revolution* (1974), Ch. 6; and A. MacLaren, *Religion and Social Class* (1974) are pioneering local studies of the bourgeoisie.

6. Thompson, op. cit., pp. 315 et seq.; Poulantzas, *Classes* ..., p. 92.

7. G. Stedman Jones, *Outcast London* (1971), part III.

8. Cf. Gramsci, op. cit., pp. 5–23, 60.

9. Foster, op. cit., is a seminal, if at times arguable, study of this process.

10. For the concept of 'organic crisis' see Gramsci, op. cit. pp. 201–11.

11. K. Marx, 'Tories and Whigs' (1852), reprinted in Marx, *Surveys from Exile*, ed. D. Fernbach, Pelican Marx Library (1973), p. 259.

12. See E. P. Hennock, *Fit and Proper Persons* (1973); T. J. Nossiter, 'Shopkeeper Radicalism in the Nineteenth Century', in T. J. Nossiter *et al.* (eds.), *Imagination and Precision in the Social Sciences* (1972).

13. See R. Harrison, *Before the Socialists* (1965), especially, pp. 113–14.

14. Poulantzas, *Classes* ..., p. 183.

15. See S. E. Finer, 'The Transmission of Benthamite Ideas', in G. Sutherland (ed.), *Studies in the Growth of Nineteenth Century Government* (1972).

16. Best, op. cit., p. 257.

17. J. S. Mill on Bentham, quoted in R. Williams, *Culture and Society*, Pelican edn. (1963), p. 72.

18. According to Gramsci every class has its own intellectuals, and the same may apply to fractions of classes: see Gramsci, op. cit., pp. 5–9.

19. Ibid., p. 261.

20. Quoted in Best, op. cit., p. 242.

21. Poulantzas, op. cit., p. 164.

22. Sutherland (ed.), op. cit., contains several illuminating studies of these variations within the civil service.
23. Anderson, op. cit.
24. This is so even where the subordinate class is largely excluded from formal participation in the polity, as the British working class was before 1867. It was nevertheless still necessary to take account of its existence as a socio-political force – not least to prevent the recurrence of militant mass protests (Chartism) against its political exclusion. It is of course true that the extension of formal political rights brought about a qualitative change in the nature of the problem.
25. This may occur, as implied in the previous note, by their representation in parties dominated by other classes; in this case the class struggle is still a political (i.e. party) struggle, with one class at a large – but never infinite – strategic advantage.
26. See especially, 'State and Civil Society', *Prison Notebooks*, pp. 206–7; cf. Poulantzas, *Classes* . . . , p. 98.
27. Gramsci, op. cit., pp. 149–50. By 'organic Party' Gramsci meant those political forms which most effectively represent the interests and organize the domination of a given social class.
28. See Fernbach's comments in his introduction to Marx, *Surveys from Exile*, pp. 18–24.
29. See, e.g. Best, op. cit., pp. 236–7.
30. See J. Vincent, *The Formation of the Liberal Party* (1966).
31. Gramsci, op. cit., p. 327.
32. L. Althusser, *For Marx*, trans. B. Brewster (1969), p. 251.
33. Gramsci, op. cit., pp. 80 (footnote), 263.
34. For this reason it seems to me mistaken to suggest, as is currently fashionable, that Gramsci's problematic has reference to bourgeois democracies (e.g. the practice under very different conditions of the Vietnamese or Spanish Communist Parties is surely exemplary from a 'Gramscian' point of view), although it is certainly true that the dimensions of the problem and the possible areas of intervention do differ.
35. Poulantzas, *Classes* . . . , p. 21.
36. See G. Stedman Jones review of Foster's book, *New Left Review* 90 (1975), pp. 54–5. This real subordination in factory industry contrasts with the formal subordinations of domestic workers (who are already wage-earners) to merchant capital; here the raw materials and finished product belong to the capitalist but the worker still has immediate command of the means of production (looms, etc.), methods and pace of work, etc. See also E. P. Thompson, 'Time, Work-discipline and Industrial Capitalism', *Past and Present* 38 (1967).
37. See R. Johnson, 'Educational Policy and Social Control', *Past and Present* 49 (1970).
38. See especially part III of Stedman Jones, *Outcast London*.
39. See L. Davidoff, 'Mastered for Life; Servant and Wife in Victorian and Edwardian England', *Journal of Social History* 7 (1974); Hobsbawm, *Age of Capital*, Ch. 13.
40. See G. Crossick, 'The Labour Aristocracy and its Values', *Victorian Studies* 19 (1976); and my book, *The Labour Aristocracy in Victorian Edinburgh* (1976), especially Chs. 5–7.
41. Cf. A. Hunt, 'Law, State and Class Struggle', *Marxism Today*, June 1976.
42. See R. Price, 'The Workingmen's Club Movement', *Victorian Studies* 15 (1971).
43. Quoted in Stedman Jones, *Outcast London*, p. 10.
44. See Gramsci, op. cit., p. 13. By 'subaltern intellectuals' Gramsci meant those strata

of 'divulgators of pre-existing, traditional, accumulated intellectual wealth' who are closely tied to the popular masses (being recruited, Gramsci points out with reference to Italy, from the peasantry and petty bourgeoisie) and function to reproduce ruling class hegemony at this social level; as the word 'subaltern' implies, Gramsci constantly uses military metaphors, in which the 'great intellectuals' are the 'general staff' and the 'subaltern intellectuals' the 'NCOs' of bourgeois hegemony.

45. The forthcoming volume of essays edited by G. Crossick, *The Lower Middle Class in Britain* (to be published by Croom Helm) attempts to open up historical discussion of these grossly neglected social groups.

46. Johnson, op. cit. pp. 117–18.

47. The function of intellectuals is to foster the cohesion and organize the domination of a given social class, to give it 'homogeneity and an awareness of its own function not only in the economic but also in the social and political fields' (Gramsci, op. cit., p. 5); groups may perform this function without being 'intellectuals' in a specific occupational sense.

48. Foster, op. cit., pp. 166–74.

49. Poulantzas, 'Marxist Political Theory . . .', p. 67.

50. Cf. M. Jacques, 'Trends in Youth Culture', *Marxism Today*, April 1975; R. Williams, 'Base and Superstructure', *New Left Review* 82 (1973), pp. 8–12.

THE CONCEPT OF CLASS IN MARXIST THEORY AND MARXIST POLITICS

BARRY HINDESS

My object in this paper is to combat 'reductionist' and 'essentialist' theoretical positions and to indicate their effects in political analysis and the determination of political strategy. For this purpose, I want to pose questions to do with the concepts of class and class struggle. I shall do this by reference to recent Marxist attempts to analyse and identify classes in contemporary capitalism, in particular to Poulantzas' *Classes in Contemporary Capitalism* and the Communist Party pamphlet *Class Structure*. My aim is to identify a serious ambiguity in traditional Marxist conceptualizations of classes and class struggle and the 'essentialist' mode of political analysis that often follows from it.

Essentialism in this context refers to a mode of analysis in which social phenomena are analysed not in terms of their specific conditions of existence and their effects with regard to other social relations and practices but rather as the more or less adequate expression of an essence. Well known examples with Marxist thought are economism, in which political forces are effectively reduced to manifestations of class interests determined at the level of the economy, and the work of Lukács, in which cultural phenomena are interpreted as more or less adequate expressions of an imputed class consciousness.

An essentialist mode of political analysis involves a *reduction* of political forces to 'interests' determined elsewhere (basically in the economy) and a political strategy that fails to take account of the specific political forces at work in the social formation in question. The paper closes with some limited proposals for the development of non-essentialist modes of political analysis.[1]

Mode of production and transition from one social formation to another

But first, to set the scene for subsequent discussion, I want to refer to a work of Marxist theory by Paul Hirst and myself, *Pre-Capitalist*

Modes of Production. What is important about that book in the present context is its critique of the essentialism of the work of Althusser and Balibar in *Reading Capital.* One of our main arguments is directed against the concept of 'structural causality' advanced by Althusser and adopted, with significant variations, by Poulantzas and many others. We argue that that concept is essentially teleological and little different in principle from the 'expressive causality'[2] which Althusser quite rightly castigates in *Reading Capital* and elsewhere.

Althusser's concept of structural causality involves a sophisticated reworking of the traditional Marxist conception (based on Marx's 1859 Preface to *A Contribution to a Critique of Political Economy*) in which a mode of production is represented as consisting of three levels (or two in the case of classless societies), the economic, political and ideological (or cultural) levels, with the economy as determinant 'in the last instance' and the other two as relatively autonomous – so that, while the political and ideological superstructures are conceived as being determined by their economic basis they are nevertheless thought to be relatively independent of it and to react back upon the economy.

In *Reading Capital,* mode of production is represented as a structure of three levels (or two) in which the economy plays a double role: first it appears as a level in the structure, and secondly it determines the character of the three levels and the relations that hold between them. In the case of the capitalist mode of production the economy is said to be both dominant and determinant, but in other modes of production politics or ideology may be dominant.[3] Althusser maintains that the three levels are related by a structural causality in the sense that each part of the structure is an effect of the structure as a whole and the whole (in this case the mode of production) is nothing other than the totality of its effects.

Thus the existence of the structure, in Althusser's view, secures the conditions of existence of its parts (as effects of the structure) and the existence of the parts is nothing other than the existence of the structure itself. Althusser therefore maintains that each mode of production must be conceived as 'eternity in Spinoza's sense' (p. 107), meaning that the mode of production secures its own conditions of existence and is therefore capable of eternal reproduction.

The position outlined very briefly here is criticized at length by Paul Hirst and myself in Chapter 6, 'The Transition from Feudalism to Capitalism', and in the Conclusion to *Pre-Capitalist Modes of*

Production. We advance the alternative proposal to conceptualize the connections between relations of production and political, legal and ideological or cultural forms and relations in terms of *conditions of existence.* This means that while, for example, certain legal forms may be necessary as conditions of existence of capitalist relations of production, their existence is not secured by capitalist relations of production themselves. Our argument on this point has two immediate consequences: first, the dissolution of the problem of transition from one mode of production to another as conceived in *Reading Capital* and in other teleological forms of Marxism, and secondly, the transformation of the area of problems concerning the position of the relations of production vis-à-vis other elements of the social formation.

The problem of transition from one mode of production to another, say from feudalism to capitalism or from capitalism to socialism, is the site of a major theoretical inconsistency in *Reading Capital* signalling the collapse of its attempt to transcend the manifest teleology that has plagued so much of Marxist theory – for example, in the conception of history as the inexorable forward march of the 'productive forces' interrupted from time to time by brief periods of intense class conflict while the lagging 'relations of production' are brought back into line.

On the one hand, Althusser and Balibar elaborate a powerful critique of teleological conceptions of Marxism which posit an inevitable evolution from one mode of production to another and, in contrast to the teleological conceptions of mode of production as essentially finite and transitory, they advance a conception of mode of production as 'eternity', that is, as a structure whose existence entails its continued reproduction.

On the other hand, Althusser and Balibar have a conception of history in which transition from one mode of production to another can and does take place.

Now, if mode of production as eternity involves a structure whose existence entails its reproduction, transition can be conceived only in terms of an entirely different structure of production, namely, one whose existence entails its own dissolution. In effect, Balibar postulates two types of structure of production: in the first, relations of production and productive forces correspond and reproduce each other, thus giving the structure of an eternity; in the second, relations and forces fail to correspond and one acts so as to transform the other, thus giving the structure of transition. This position has the merit of providing a clear conception of transition and of explaining why a period of transition must come to an end: transition brings together in a single structure of production the *relations* of one mode of production and the forces of another, and it comes to an end because the relations transform the forces – for examples, the transition from feudalism to capitalism ends in capitalism because the capitalist relations of production transform the *feudal* forces of production into *capitalist* ones.

So far so good. But the major inconsistency remains, for if mode of production is indeed an *eternity* it must follow that transition from one mode of production to another is impossible. How is it possible to get out of an eternity, say the feudal mode of production, into a period of transition, say from feudalism to capitalism? That problem cannot be resolved within the framework of *Reading Capital*. If mode of production is an eternity, then transition is impossible. If transition is possible, then mode of production cannot be conceived as an eternity. In effect, Althusser and Balibar displace the manifest teleology of evolutionary forms of Marxism in favour of a logically impossible combination in which periods of transition, conceived teleologically, link modes of production, conceived as eternities.

In *Pre-Capitalist Modes of Production* we contrasted the teleological causality of *Reading Capital* and of evolutionist conceptions in which the productive forces 'inevitably come into conflict with' relations of production with the material causality of the class struggle. If transition from one mode of production to another takes place, we argued, that is not a teleological function of the structure of the mode of production itself, nor of Balibar's 'forms of transition'. Rather it is a function of the material causality of the class struggle. That is to say, it is the outcome of conflict between definite political forces. This is fine as far as it goes, but there remains a problem with regard to this conception of 'class struggle'. I'll return to that in a moment.

The second consequence concerns the position of the relations of production vis-à-vis other elements of the social formation. It involves the dissolution of that whole set of problems generated by the notion of the determination 'in the last instance' of other social relations by the economy. Examples here are the problems of how to reconcile *determination* by the economy with the autonomy of other social relations, or how to make sense of the concept of 'relative autonomy', a concept which illustrates the contradiction perfectly by affirming that while political and cultural relations are autonomous from the economy they are only relatively so. This concept is heavily used by Poulantzas who tries hard to have it both ways. That set of problems must be replaced by a different set of problems which concern the conditions of existence of determinate relations of production. Rather than conceive of mode of production and social formation in terms of an economic base 'upon which' other structural levels (rise), it is necessary to conceptualize social formation as a social form in which the conditions of existence of determinate relations of production are secured. For example, 'feudal social formation' refers to a social form in which the political, legal and cultural conditions of existence of feudal relations of production are met. But the concept of feudal relations of production does not give us the particular forms in which those conditions will be met. At the most it allows us to determine whether particular political, legal and other forms are compatible or incompatible with the maintenance of feudal relations of production. The significance of this consequence will be considered in the final part of this paper.

Classes and politics

To return to the concepts of class and class struggle, the main point I want to make in this paper is that there is a basic ambiguity in classical Marxist treatments of classes and class relations.

On the one hand, classes are defined in economic terms as a function of determinate relations of production,[4] as categories of economic agents who either possess or are separated from the means of production – bourgeoisie and proletariat, lord and serf, slave-owner and slave, etc. On the other hand, classes are conceived as participants in political and ideological struggle in the sense that classes are, or are represented by, political forces and ideological forms. The ambiguity here concerns the problem of reconciling the notion of classes as categories of economic agents, political forces, and ideological forms – that is, the *unity* of a class in these three aspects – with a non-reductionist conception of the autonomy of political and ideological forces with regard to the relations of production.

Now, the autonomy of political and ideological forces is widely acknowledged in classical Marxist political analyses. To give just one example, in *The Agrarian Programme of Social Democracy in the First Russian Revolution* Lenin insists that the balance of political forces cannot be deduced from the structure of economic relations. The problem concerns the consequences of the recognition of that autonomy for the conceptualization of classes and class relations. If politics and ideology are not to be conceived as mere epiphenomena of the economy, then what constitutes the unity of classes in these three aspects? What mechanisms define and ensure the articulation of political-legal forces and ideological-cultural forms on to the classes they are alleged to represent? It is clear that once we acknowledge that autonomy (however 'relative'), then the unity of classes as economic, political-legal and ideological-cultural agencies must be problematic. Hence for *Pre-Capitalist Modes of Production* to insist on the material causality of the class struggle is less than fully informative.

Now, to show that these points are not merely academic and to bring out their political significance let me comment briefly on two recent Marxist texts on classes, the Communist Party pamphlet *Class Structure* and Poulantzas' book *Classes in Contemporary Capitalism*. Both texts are political, at least in intention, and both insist on the political importance of a correct analysis of classes in contemporary capitalism. They are particularly concerned with the problems posed for Marxist political practice by the so-called middle-strata, Poulantzas' 'new petty-bourgeoisie'. For example, Poulantzas sees the French Communist Party's position on the 'middle-strata' as grounds for a savage political attack (e.g. p. 204). He argues, in effect, that if you don't get their class determination, and therefore their class interests, right then serious political errors must follow. This is not the place to analyse these texts in any detail. Instead I shall simply note a few significant features of each text and then add some more general remarks.

First, consider two extracts from the pamphlet *Class Structure*. In his article 'Perspectives for Class Struggle and Alliances' Sam Aaronovitch refers to the political forces that may come together against bourgeois society:

> The nature of the issues posed by contemporary capitalism brings into action (or can do so) a series of *intersecting forces* which comprise: various sections of the working class as broadly defined; non-proletarian classes and 'transitional' elements (self-employed tradesmen and small producers); social and 'interest' groupings (such as students, women, parents, tenants of councils and private landlords); political parties and groups (such as the political parties and groups on the left, the Young Liberals, some anti-Common Market organisations, etc.).

The point to notice about this list of forces is that the working class appears twice: first as itself and secondly in the shape of the organized parties and groupings which represent it. Thus the working class *exists as a political force* independently of the 'political parties and groups on the left' which represent it. A similar list later in the same article presents the working class as a political force distinct from 'political parties and economic organizations of the working people'.

The second extract comes from Jack Cohen's 'Some Thoughts on the Working Class Today'. Cohen gives a definition of the working class which begins with their position in relation to the means of production and then continues:

> whose interests are therefore absolutely opposed to those of the owners of the means of production, the capitalists, and who are therefore driven to struggle continually in defence of their immediate interests and for the long-term overthrow of the capitalist system of exploitation.

This definition contains an implicit recognition that politics cannot be reduced to classes. It defines a *direction* in which working-class political practice is supposed to evolve, namely, towards a political practice based on the self-conscious attempt to realize the objective interests given by its class position. At any given time therefore, so long as that evolution is incomplete, working-class politics must contain features that are not reducible to class position. Thus Cohen admits that political forces are not reducible to class interests and utterly fails to conceptualize the difference except in teleological form.

Now consider Poulantzas' book *Classes in Contemporary Capitalism*. Apart from the general problems connected with his use of the notion of structural causality and from the manifest circularity of the relation he posits between structure and class practice,[5] there are also serious problems in his conceptualization of classes and political and ideological forces. Two types of position are particularly instructive.

First, in Poulantzas' view class determination is an effect of the structure (i.e. of political and ideological determinations as well as economic ones) and it is this that defines class interests. But class *interests*, determined by the structure, are not necessarily equivalent to class *positions* taken in particular concrete situations (conjunctures). Hence the structure of the social formation gives class determinations which define class interests and the political and ideological positions which correspond to those interests. But in any particular conjuncture the position taken by a class may differ from its interests and Poulantzas insists that there is no necessity for class position to correspond to class determination:

> We must rid ourselves once and for all of the illusions that have often affected the revolutionary movement, throughout its history, to the effect that an objective proletarian polarization of class determinations must necessarily lead in time to a polarization of class positions. (p. 334)

We therefore have the following paradox. On the one hand, his whole analysis of the 'middle-strata' is aimed at establishing their class determination and he insists that that is of the greatest political importance and launches a vitriolic attack on the French Communist Party for getting it wrong. On the other hand, he maintains that there is no reason to suppose that class position will correspond to that determination – and *that* suggests that the establishment of class determination is of no political significance at all. In effect, we are presented with a reduction of politics and ideology to class determinations, as effects of the structure, coupled with an acknowledgement of the irreducibility of politics and ideology to class determinations, as effects of the conjuncture. But Poulantzas gives no account of how it is possible for effects of conjunctures to differ from those of structures nor of what connections, if any, obtain between them.

Secondly, in discussing political apparatuses Poulantzas tells us that they are 'never anything other than the materialization and condensation of class relations' (p. 25). For example:

> The State is not an 'entity' with an intrinsic instrumental essence, but it is itself a relation, more precisely the condensation of a relation. (p. 26)

Here again we have the reduction of politics to classes (apparatuses are *nothing other than . . .*) coupled with the denegation of that reduction (they materialize and condense those relations and therefore differ according to the forms of 'materialization' and 'condensation').

These texts provide clear illustrations of the effects of the traditional Marxist ambiguity with regard to classes: on the one hand politics and ideology are effects of class determinations, and on the other hand they are not. The result is that in spite of an explicit and manifest concern with politics these texts produce little more than a more or less complex economism involving both the recognition and the denial of the autonomy of politics and ideology vis-à-vis the economy.

An index of this weakness is the manifest failure of these analyses to get to grips with politics in Britain or France and their tendency to reduce political strategy, in so far as they have anything to say about it, to a simple deduction from what is thought to be the structure of the economy.

For example, the problem of the class determination of the 'middle-strata' or the 'new petty-bourgeoisie' is presented as being of the greatest importance for Marxist political stategy, but it is discussed without reference to the distinctive *political* features of Britain, France, West Germany, etc.

Or again, consider the 'strategy' of anti-monopoly alliance. Sam Aaronovitch's paper shows how the essential features of this 'strategy' may be derived simply from the fact of monopoly capitalism and without reference to any analysis of politics. Monopoly capitalism, he argues, means the concentration of economic power by the bourgeoisie and within that class by big capital as against small and medium capital. Big business is dominant but numerically small and the concentration of economic power in its hands is manifestly anti-democratic and detrimental to the interests of other sections of the bourgeoisie, the petty-bourgeoisie, the working class and a wide range of social groupings and forces. Hence the strategy: anti-monopoly alliance brings together the broad mass of the people against the small minority of big capitalists.

Poulantzas' position on the significance of monopoly capitalism and his polemics against this strategy depend on a different analysis of the economic relations between monopoly capital and other fractions of the capitalist class. But what is striking about this strategy and Poulantzas' attack on it is that both positions are derived from a more or less sophisticated analysis of the structure of economic relations. Here again the main features of the *political* strategy of anti-monopoly alliance are discussed quite independently of any analysis of the particular and distinctive *political* features of Britain, France, etc. In effect, and despite at least a partial recognition of the irreducibility of politics to class determinations, political strategy is treated as a simple consequence of the interests of classes and class fractions and these are defined by class determinations and the structure of the economy.

Class relations and political forces

These consequences illustrate the theoretical fragility of the notion of the 'relative autonomy' of politics and ideology. *Either* we effectively reduce political and ideological phenomena to class interests determined elsewhere (basically in the economy) – i.e. an economic reductionism coupled with a vague recognition that things are actually more complicated and a failure to get to grips with that complication. *Or* we must face up to the real autonomy of political and ideological phenomena and their irreducibility to manifestations of interests determined by the structure of the economy.

The first alternative has been illustrated above. The second brings us back to the second consequence of the critique of structural causality noted in the first part of this paper, namely, that relations of production have determinate political-legal and ideological-cultural conditions of existence but those conditions are not secured by or generated by the relations of production themselves. This means that political and legal forces and ideological and cultural forms cannot be conceived as reducible to the 'representation' of classes and class interests. In other words, if we define classes in terms of positions defined with regard to determinate relations of production, then we cannot also maintain the reduction of political and ideological phenomena to effects of those classes and their 'objective' interests.

How, then, are we to conceptualize the connections between relations of production and, say, political and legal phenomena?

Consider, for example, capitalist relations of production and the wage-labour contracts, enterprises, money, etc., which they involve. To say that capitalist relations of production involve wage-labour contracts is to say that the wage-labour relation presupposes legal recognition of the form of contract and that implies the *possibility* of a variety of legal determinations of the conditions of contract (minimum wages, hours, conditions of employment, redundancy and pension rights, etc.). The point about all of these is that they are *possible* but not *necessary*, given capitalist relations of production. But the wage-labour contract must always be *determinate* in the sense that a contract always specifies definite conditions and obligations on the parties to that contract. There must always be some legal specification of the forms of contract that are possible and of those that are precluded by law and, within those limits, each wage-labour contract presupposes some further determination of the particular conditions that are specified in the contract. These conditions of contract are determined, not by capitalist relations of production (which on this point require only that there be determinate wage-labour contracts), but by the effects of the struggle of definite social forces acting, in the case of legal regulation, on the legislative and juridical apparatuses of the state. Capitalist relations of production presuppose legal regulation of contract as their condition of existence but they do not determine the form that regulation takes.

Similarly, wage-labour presupposes a definite wage-level or system of wage-levels. At any given time wages are fixed at such-and-such a level, neither more nor less. These levels are not determined by features of the economy alone, by relations of production and the technical conditions of production, but also by the intervention of political, legal and cultural determinations. Wage-labour, in other words, presupposes some definite legal recognition and legal regulation of the conditions of contract and some definite level or levels of wages. It therefore presupposes the existence of social forces whose struggle has the effect of determining those conditions and levels. Where there are capitalist relations of production there must be conflicting political forces.

Or again, if we consider the capitalist enterprise it is clear that it must be an entity capable of entering into contractual relations with workers, with other enterprises, etc. Hence the existence of an enterprise requires that it be legally recognized as an entity capable of contracting to purchase and to supply commodities. Capitalism therefore presupposes legal definitions of forms of incorporation of enterprises, partnerships, limited and unlimited companies, etc., legal specification of the conditions of formation of limited liability companies, and so on – and those conditions clearly affect the scale of operation that is possible. Legal recognition of definite forms of incorporation of business enterprises does not merely codify pre-existing forms of capitalist organization. On the contrary, the presence of the appropriate legal forms is an indispensable condition of the formation of the joint-stock company as a business enterprise.

Once again, capitalist relations of production presuppose the legal recognition of some forms of enterprise but they do not tell us what forms will be recognized or what legal constraints they will suffer.

These examples, of the wage-labour relation and of the enterprise, illustrate the point that capitalist relations of production do require definite political-legal and ideological or cultural conditions of existence but that they do not determine the precise form in which their conditions of existence will be secured. Those forms may be modified by the struggle of social forces, and the persistence in any form of the conditions of existence of, capitalist relations *may* also be subject to the effects of that struggle.

Where there are capitalist relations there must also be conflicting social forces whose struggle provides definite conditions necessary to the existence of capitalist relations – since there must be some definite forms of legal regulation, definite levels of wages, and so on. But those forces cannot be reduced to effects or reflections of economic class relations.

This means that there are political forces not directly tied to economic class relations, from the National Council for Civil Liberties to the organizations of the women's movement, and that they have real effects which need to be considered in the determination of political strategy. Further, since politics do not simply reflect economic class relations, it means that the working class is not automatically or essentially socialist, that working-class politics are not automatically progressive – consider the example of the USA where the conditions of wage-labour and the levels of wages are now determined without the intervention of any significant socialist forces, or the manifest weakness of serious socialist politics in Britain.

While the existence of capitalist relations of production requires that there be determinate forms of wage-labour contract, of enterprise, levels of wage-payment, etc., and therefore requires that these forms be determinate effects of political, legal and ideological forces, there is nothing in capitalist relations of production themselves to ensure that any of those forces will be or will tend to become socialist. Forces have to be won for socialism, they will not simply fall into our laps, and the identification of classes and class fractions cannot in itself provide the foundation for any serious political strategy.

NOTES

1. The positions advanced in this paper depend on arguments which cannot be fully developed here. Some of these arguments are elaborated at greater length in a forthcoming paper by Paul Hirst and me which corrects and develops some of our arguments in *Pre-Capitalist Modes of Production* and in other future publications.

2. Expressive causality is a form of essentialism defined by Althusser as follows:
    'This is the model that dominates all Hegel's thought. But it presupposes in principle that the whole in question be reducible to an *inner essence*, of which the elements of the whole are then no more than the phenomenal forms of expression, the inner principle of the essence being present at each point in the whole, such that at each moment it is possible to write the immediately adequate equation: *such and such an element* (economic, political, legal, literary, religious, etc., in Hegel) = *the inner essence of the whole' (Reading Capital*, pp. 186–7).
    Paul Hirst and I have shown that structural causality is merely another form of expressive causality.

3. This manner of distinguishing between capitalism and other modes of production appears in many of Marx's comments. For example, in a much quoted footnote to *Capital*, Vol. 1 Marx replies to a critic who argues that, while it may be true that 'the mode of production determines the character of the social, political, and intellectual life generally' in capitalist society, other areas of life are dominant in other societies. Marx comments:
    'This much, however, is clear that the middle ages could not live on Catholicism, nor the ancient world on politics. On the contrary, it is the economic conditions of the time that explain why here politics and there Catholicism play the chief part' (p. 86n).
    Here there appears to be a distinction between two kinds of relation between levels, determination 'in the last instance' and 'playing the chief part'. Althusser refers to these as determination and dominance.

4. Some Marxists have suggested that pre-capitalist relations of production are political and legal in form rather than directly economic. A recent example of such an argument can be found in the Conclusion to P. Anderson, *Lineages of the Absolutist State*. Paul Hirst and I have shown that that position confuses relations of production on the one hand and their political-legal conditions of existence on the other. See especially *Pre-Capitalist Modes of Production*, Chapter 5.

5. For example: 'the effectiveness of the structure on the field of practices is itself limited by the intervention of political practice on the structure' (*Political Power and Social Classes*, p. 95).

BEYOND SPONTANEITY

GERRY LEVERSHA

I propose to discuss the Leninist theory of the Revolutionary Party in the light of the ideas of Antonio Gramsci. Lenin's conception of leadership is not without its ambiguities, and some of these have become especially problematical in relation to contemporary conditions.

The principal question at issue concerns the tension inherent in the very concept of leadership. How do you keep in contact with the people's level of understanding, while at the same time aiming to increase it in a desired direction? There are twin faults to which revolutionaries have always been prone; *spontaneism* – effectively denying the need for leadership by a passive acceptance of people's immediate consciousness – and *voluntarism* – over-estimating the actual state of popular understanding, and cutting oneself off from the masses by insisting upon a purist 'correct' line. In the one case the Party degenerates into a rearguard, in the other into a sect. Other problems which arise are: what should the composition of the Party be? how should it relate to the broad movement? how does its function change with the progress of the revolution?

The aim of this paper is to discuss these questions, and the responses first of the Bolshevik Party, led by Lenin, and then of Gramsci, in the context of the whole revolutionary strategy. There is evidently a continuity between Gramsci's conceptions of the Party and its role and those of Lenin – an identity of standpoint on profounder points of Lenin's conception of the Party. At the same time, it is quite unrealistic for socialists in the West today to try to repeat the Russian experience of 1917, either in the tactics adopted or in the kind of organization envisaged.

Gramsci on spontaneity and conscious organization

For nine years the Italian Communist leader Antonio Gramsci was incarcerated by the Mussolini regime in the prison at Turi, his release, due to illness, occurring a year before his death. Throughout this period he kept in contact with the outside world only by reading books and by exchanging letters with his family and close friends. The correspondence has survived intact, and has been acknowledged as one of the triumphs of Italian twentieth-century literature, as well as a moving testimonial to a courageous socialist. As we read it, we realize that Gramsci, prevented for reasons of censorship from explicit political analysis (save in his secret Notebooks), was dwelling upon seemingly trivial details of his personal life, and in so doing, was bringing his politician's mind to bear on 'non-political' problems. In one letter to his wife Giulia, he is criticizing her for the way in which she is overseeing the educational development of their son Delio. Superficially, his remarks which warn against the dangers of spontaneous development of Delio's personality, might seem to have a lot in common with Black Paper sentiments; but as the argument develops we recognize that he is really displaying an acute understanding of the way in which the 'impersonal' forces of society mould individual character and consciousness:

> To refuse to 'form' the child merely means allowing him to pick up the motifs of life chaotically from his general environment, and letting his personality develop in a haphazard way. . . . What is believed to be latent force is actually . . . nothing but the inchoate and indistinct complex of images and sense-impressions of the first days . . . that are not always the best that could be imagined. . . .[1]

In other words, the result of leaving an individual to the mercy of chance influence is, more often than not, the formation of a selfish, conformist, narrow-minded and unimaginative person. There is no such thing in life as 'pure spontaneity'.

What is true of the individual is, in this case, truer still of the social organism. The sentiment above is not really very original, except in its mode of expression: it stems from certain often misunderstood theses of historical materialism, previously emphasized by Lenin.[2] They bear upon the nature of 'ideology' – our conception of the world and our place in it – which plays a crucial role in the historical process, and cannot be dismissed as a blind reflection of economic forces. Marx explained how the basis of ideology is our 'social practice'; ideology is our 'lived relation to the world'.[3] One cannot explain away our consciousness as a 'false consciousness' which is the result of a confidence trick pulled by 'them'; it has an objective necessity and it encircles 'them' too. History is not a huge conspiracy.

However, the tenor of the Marxist theory of ideology is that, if we are not careful, we may ignore the fact that our ideas flow largely from processes which we do not control, and this may prove a major stumbling block to our revolutionary practice. Let us look at a number of examples. The spontaneous reaction of a child brought up to see father relaxing in front of the telly every night after work whilst mum slaves away in the kitchen is captured by the slogan: 'A woman's place is in the home!' Similarly, the famous expression of economistic reformism – 'A fair day's pay for a fair day's work' – is a spontaneous reaction to everyday exploitation in the workplace, and is crystallized in the wages struggle which accepts the competitive framework of the capitalist market. The point is that what we would call a *revolutionary* consciousness – one which challenges the sexual division of labour in the home, or the wages system itself – develops only through the conscious intervention of some 'intellectual agency' from 'outside' which sees further than the immediate present, understanding history in its entirety rather than in its superficial aspect. For the Leninist tradition this agency is the Party.

The problem at the centre of the theory of the Party is that of what form the conscious and organized force should take in order to be most effective in recommending to the class the strategy and tactics for the seizure of State power and the construction of a communist society. The problem must be resolved in the twin knowledge that class ideology – by its very nature – cannot be altered either automatically, by the growth of 'objective' factors on their own, or by the mere existence of an omniscient élite who preach truth from pulpits set up away from the class's everyday experience. The dilemma must be reconciled, somehow.

Lenin and the Revolutionary Party

When he formulated the doctrine of the Revolutionary Party, Lenin was wont to justify its necessity *negatively*, by reference to various tendencies within the workers' movement which failed to grasp the correct relation between spontaneous ideology and historical knowledge.

The *anarchists* worshipped spontaneity in itself, as the guarantee of the revolutionary process and as the key to the organization of society as a whole. A politics of pure protest would usher in a new society, governed directly by producers without the intermediary of a State machine, and characterized by the gradual growth of co-operative forms of ownership and control progressively eliminating individual capitalist institutions. There could be no place in this scheme for a centralized authoritarian Party.[4]

The *economists*[5] denied any active role to the superstructure, understanding history as a process of straightforward evolution from lower to higher forms of social organization, impelled by the irresistible dynamic of the forces of production. Since the speed and course of this process was only marginally affected by conscious intervention, the notion of an activist Party was redundant, and the existing forms of political organization (the trade unions and social-democratic parties) could fulfil the technical, essentially administrative function of directing the class according to the economic situation.

The third of these conceptions, which I call *Jacobinism*, expressed its exasperation with the pessimistic conclusions of economic determinism by an irrational glorification of the individual act. For those such as Blanqui, a party could not hope to bring any consciousness to a mass doomed to sluggish passivity. Leadership was to be confined to a conspiratorial élite, who would carry off brilliant coups which might overturn the existing order and accelerate the course of history.

No more then than now did these tendencies appear in a 'pure' form. They are rather constituents of a whole spectrum of attitudes towards leadership. Lenin's theoretical breakthrough was to discern a shared origin to these diverging attitudes: the reduction of the historical process to the unfolding of a predetermined drama enacted by a subject. In a strong sense all three recipes for revolution were variations upon a theme. For anarchism, the scattered mass stumbles on blindly towards the communist horizon, which they will reach by means of the accumulation of a myriad random motions. For economism, the insensible class is guided onwards by the unseen but reliable hand of productivity. For Jacobinism, the ignorant multitude drifts on slumbering through the intermittent heroics of the chosen few. In all three scenarios the star actors perform, blindfold, a prewritten screenplay.

Lenin argues in opposition that history cannot be so conceived. The outcome of the drama is not determined before the curtain rises, but is vitally affected by the actors' performances. They do not have to ad lib any more than they have to see the script beforehand, but if they are to co-ordinate their roles, and understand the significance of each scene in context, they need a director. This director is the revolutionary Party.

Following Kautsky, Lenin maintained that revolutionary consciousness had to be imported into the working class from outside its everyday life activity. But in borrowing this thesis, Lenin shifted certain of the emphases. First, it was not to imply that only 'bourgeois intellectuals' could lead the revolution; the reference is to an intellectual *function* – that of being able to evaluate a situation in terms of a scientific theory which has implications beyond the immediate context of the situation – rather than to the class positions or origins of the carriers of scientific knowledge. It is nonetheless true that, by the very nature of the division of labour in capitalist society, the intellectuals would at first tend to hail from the old ruling classes or petty bourgeoisie, and thus be betraying their own class origins by placing their abilities at the service of the proletariat. Secondly, we return to the perennial problem of how the Party is to *relate to* the daily experience of the workers, while remaining 'critical' of it.

In order to discharge its duties effectively, the Leninist party evolved in a certain shape, conforming to a number of characteristics which defined it.

First, it was to be a *vanguard* Party, way out ahead of popular intuition in its theory and overall strategic understanding, as a bulwark against a regression to spontaneism. Theoretically, this meant an explicit adherence to Marxism as an 'official' theory, recognizing clearly the dynamic of capitalism and the nature of the political State, in order to analyse the concrete conjuncture at any instant, including the needs and aspirations of all classes and sectors in society, and thence derive guidelines to action.

Secondly, the Party needed the fullest *internal democracy*, to permit debate amongst its membership, and ensure the political development and real commitment of its cadre force. Taking these two characteristics together, we have the notion of Party as *collective intellectual*.

Thirdly, to lend it the authority and co-ordination for action in accordance with its analysis, the Party needed to be *disciplined*. This made the element of democracy even more crucial, in order to prevent the Party from degenerating into a purely military apparatus, with an élite hierarchy and a robot-like mass, automatically obeying orders it had no part in formulating. These elements were to be fused in the contradictory unity of '*democratic centralism*'.

Finally, to earn it respect among non-party workers, and to ensure the fullest possible contact with the class it was to lead, the Party had to nurture and maintain a *proletarian* composition. That was not to say that it should not contain non-proletarian cadres – this was essential in view of its intellectual function – but that an eventual numerical bias in favour of the working class should be attained.

The Bolsheviks and their critics

The Bolshevik Party developed in the particular conditions of Russian society in the first two decades of this century, and it would be against all Marxist principles to ignore the effect which its specific adolescence had upon the way in which it translated into reality Lenin's doctrines. In a country where the working class constituted only a small minority of the population, in a total absence of democratic traditions and freedoms, under the iron heel of Tsarist autocracy, amid a people locked in feudal and patriarchal attitudes, the Bolsheviks were a tiny élite party, led by petty bourgeois intellectuals who had spent most of the pre-revolutionary years in exile, with almost no support from the peasantry and then only for its most populist slogans. Reared in conditions of clandestinity, it relied far more upon unquestioned obedience than on equal debate. Even on the eve of the revolution, it is doubtful whether more than a handful of Lenin's closest supporters on the Central Committee understood the originality of the April Theses.[6]

All these tendencies were exaggerated after the Revolution by the terrible years of civil war and economic recovery.[7] By Lenin's death in 1924, the Party had assumed a monolithic isolated quality beyond all the initial intention. Attempts to inject new adrenalin into the Soviet system failed as it became clear that small-capitalist ideology held sway amongst the rural masses.[8] Inner-party debate developed into confrontations between official and 'dissident' lines, with a resulting personification of real conflicts in society, which helped to lay the basis for 'Stalinism'. The leadership recognized the existence of the dilemma but could not find a solution; Trotsky in particular never really understood the *objective* problems of bureaucratization. With the call at the Fifth Congress of the Comintern in 1924 for the 'Bolshevization' of all member parties, a virtue was made of the Soviet necessity, and a single mode of organization recommended as a universal panacea. Features such as monolithism and proletarian purity were imposed on parties for which they were quite unsuitable, especially when Comintern policy became increasingly centralized. Some parties – for instance, the Chinese – suffered disastrously.

One alternative open to revolutionary theory was to reject the basic premises of 'What is to be done?'; this was the line taken by several Marxists during Lenin's lifetime, most prominent among whom was Rosa Luxemburg. She accused Lenin of Blanquism for his insistence on a centralized vanguard, and for his contention that a theoretical opposition to opportunism had to be reinforced by an organizational autonomy.[9] She believed that she had proved, through considerations on Marx's reproduction theory,[10] that the final and inevitable crisis of capitalism would lead to a spontaneous radicalization of the masses ushering in either socialism or an era of barbarism, requiring only the existence of revolutionary fractions inside the socialist parties to exert the needed pressure at the vital moment. Holding, moreover, that class alliances and nationalist struggles were superfluous and indeed diversionary, Rosa criticized the Bolsheviks for their restraining and disciplining influence in the post-revolutionary period.[11] But her optimism proved tragically unfounded as the initial successes of the German workers' movement – on which Lenin himself placed an excessive reliance – declined into a welter of adventurism and opportunism, and witnessed the murders of Luxemburg and Liebknecht.

Rosa's anti-Leninism was carried to its logical extreme by the Dutch council-communist Anton Pannekoek. For him communist construction required the dismantling of the political party per se and a total reliance on autonomous working-class organizations, and therefore Lenin was but the final representative of the authoritarian death throes of capitalist society.[12] Pannekoek headed a libertarian current which has borne little fruit inside the Marxist movement; it is sadly ironic to hear his latter-day apologists, such as Paul Mattick, bemoaning the immaturity of a working class which cannot recognize, in his doctrines, its own spontaneous impulses.

Both the critiques above were based on pure spontaneism, and thus failed from the outset to tackle the real and pressing problems of what kind of revolutionary leadership fitted 'Western' conditions, with a long tradition of bourgeois representative democracy and a strong industrial working class. If we want clarification as to whether the Leninist hypothesis is inappropriate in its essentials for this task, or whether the principles can be retained though dressed in new garb, we can do no better than return to that convinced anti-spontaneist, Antonio Gramsci.

Gramsci's concept of 'hegemony'

There are striking similarities between the early political development of Gramsci and the work of Rosa Luxemburg; the concern with workers' councils, the distrust of sectarianism, the emphasis upon the act of will – to the extent that, for Gramsci, the Bolshevik October was the 'revolution *against* Das Kapital'![13] But the Italian thinker, with his rejection of pure spontaneity, was marked out from the first as the more profound politician.

In his articles for the magazine *L'Ordine Nuovo*, which appeared during the 'Red Two Years' of the Turin factory occupations, Gramsci was preoccupied by the relationships between the workers' councils, the trade unions, and the Socialist party, of which he was, like all other Italian Marxists, a member.[14] The role of the unions – that of waging the spontaneous wage struggle *within* the ideological frame of capitalism – he counterposed to the *constructive* function of the councils, anticipating the time when the working class would assume direction of society.

Gramsci recognized that the councils would not form themselves into an efficiently functioning State structure on a national basis without the growth of socialist consciousness, and looked to the Socialist Party as the force for change. This was a party torn by factional struggle; on the one hand there was a reformist right, on the other an abstentionist group led by Amadeo Bordiga, and in the 'centre' a majority exhibiting the phenomenon of 'maximalism' – verbal adherence to the programme of the Third International coupled with practical passivity.[15] Despite his isolation, Gramsci was loath to promote a Communist fraction, for he knew that in any split to the left, the Turin group would find itself submerged by Bordiga's influence. The latter faction labelled Gramsci an idealist and syndicalist, underestimated the significance of the workers' councils, and based their politics on sectarian purism and outright dismissal of the parliamentary struggle. Gramsci's lateness in accepting Leninist concepts of the party can be partly attributed to the antipathy he felt towards Bordiga, who, for him, *represented* Leninism.

But in addition he was already disturbed by detecting certain Jacobin traits in the Bolshevik experience, not only in what he viewed as attempts to bring all the spontaneity of the masses under the direct custody of the Party, but also in the measures – dictated by the Russian conditions – which led to the substitution of Party for State, and encouraged the phenomenon of 'statolatry' – the excessive worship of State repressive forms – which looked as if it might become a permanent rather than a transitional feature of the Soviet model.[16]

In 1920, in the occupation of the factories, workers of Turin found themselves abandoned by a class-collaborationist Socialist Party, and, the break being inevitable, the Communist Party of Italy was formed. For two years Gramsci found himself in a minority grouping of a party dominated by ultra-leftism. Not until after spending a further two years working in Moscow for the Comintern, did Gramsci return to Italy to replace the arrested Bordiga as leader of the Party. By now he was fully committed to the concepts of Bolshevization, as well as to the victorious faction in the Soviet inner-party dispute. Only as a prisoner of fascism was he able to reflect fully upon the Italian and Soviet experiences, and to produce a mature critique of the form of Leninism which had developed in practice.

Gramsci's 'theory of the Party' therefore appears in the *Notebooks* only in an abstract and ambiguous form, employing all manner of elliptic metaphor to escape the attentions of the prison censor. Before we can outline the main elements of his thinking on this issue, we need to sketch some other facets of his political theory.

His essentially new concept is that of *hegemony*. This is emphatically not a 'culturalist' concept – as many on the American New Left have interpreted it[17] – drifting around somewhere in the ethereal heights of alternative lifestyle 'politics', but a firmly materialist one relating to the social relations of power in society, and in particular to the means whereby the ruling class maintains its domination over the oppressed classes (as also over the other classes in the ruling bloc) without recourse to blatant repression.[18] It is therefore linked to the way in which the interests of the dominant class are represented ideologically as those of society as a whole, and to the organization of consent to this end. The consent does not spring from the action of a 'class subject' pulling invisible strings, but derives from the effects of political and ideological structures inside society and the levels of the class struggle. Hegemony is constructed and reproduced inside a web of *institutions* which Gramsci calls 'civil society', to distinguish them from the repressive aspect of the State.

It should be clearly understood that the use of the dichotomy repressive State/civil society, or the use of similar pairs such as force/consent, is not meant to imply that there are some State apparatuses which are purely repressive and that the rest are purely ideological, nor that class struggles against the State can concentrate exclusively upon one or other of these aspects. Every State structure has both its repressive and its ideological function, but some are more repressive and some more ideological than others. For example, the 'repressive' standing army has a subordinate ideological function of preserving norms of hierarchical authority, especially significant in time of war. The legal system is a delicate balance in which ideological functions probably predominate. State education has a subsidiary repressive role. In addition, civil society extends outside the 'public' State sector into the complex of private institutions – the trade unions, political parties, churches, family, etc.[19]

Ruling class hegemony is elaborated in a *theoretical* form by intellectuals; besides the 'traditional' intellectual strata this category includes technicians, business administrators, civil servants, etc., as new kinds of 'organic' intellectuals tied to a particular economic organization of society.[20] It would be wrong, however, to fall into the trap of seeing the intellectual as a tool of the ruling élite 'imposing' hegemony upon society; for hegemony arises, rather, largely *spontaneously*, in everyday life experience. Intellectuals provide the *link* between the immediate experience of the masses and the national cultural tradition; 'organic' intellectuals mediate between the productive activity of the working people and the ruling class's controlling administrative function over the labour process.

Gramsci maintained that in Russia, the Communist Party had faced a State structure which relied predominantly upon the repressive aspects of domination, whereas the Western bourgeoisie held a strong hegemonic influence over the workers due to the more highly developed system of civil society.[21] Taking this into account, the task for revolutionaries in the West was different from that allotted to the Bolsheviks in 1917.

In addition, Gramsci recognized that the problem of hegemony extended into the phase of transition to communism, and concluded that it was necessary to produce socialist intellectuals, specialized in the administration of a planned economy and the elaboration of a new popular culture, as part of the task of constructing working-class hegemony.[22]

Implied here is criticism of the limits of October, for focusing on *negative* slogans – such as 'smashing the State' and 'breaking down the old order' – at the expense of providing a (non-utopian) vision of the future constructive task. Once the Tsarist State was overturned, and especially after the repulsion of imperialist intervention, there remained a gap which could only be filled by the employment of unreliable 'experts'. The loyalty of the peasantry could only be ensured by recourse to compromise measures and bribery – as exemplified by Bukharin's slogan 'Enrich yourselves'.[23] In such an environment the only guarantee of the permanence of the revolution was a purified, élite Party dedicated to a rigid line. In the same terms Gramsci accounted for the relative ease with which fascism triumphed in his own country, as a result of the inability of a sectarian Communist Party to capture the imagination of the masses, especially the non-proletarian masses, by posing healthy long- and short-term political alternatives.

Fusing the two analyses above – the characterization of bourgeois dominance in advanced capitalism as largely hegemonic, and the constructive mission of a Communist Party in transitional periods – we arrive at the Gramscian strategy of the 'war of position'; the progressive capture of the terrain of bourgeois hegemony, breaking down the apparatus of consent, forcing the gradual isolation of the ruling class, creating an ever clearer and more convincing image of the working people as the true 'saviours of society'.[24]

In this picture, there is a massive shift of emphasis away from insurrectionism – awaiting and preparing for the great day when the bastion of power is taken by storm – towards the notion of a continual struggle on all fronts. This is not to say that a showdown, in which the ruling class resorts to naked aggression, will not occur; it leaves the options open, but stresses the primacy of political and ideological considerations over purely military ones,[25] and notes the possibility of 'peaceful' forms of transition. Nor does it imply that the revolutionary process will be 'gradual' in the sense of a smooth haul to communism by progressive accumulation of positions. Development would be uneven, involving both advances and retreats, with elements of the 'pre-revolutionary' and 'post-revolutionary' phases existing side by side.

Machiavelli had exhorted his fictional Prince to become acquainted with the science of politics. For Gramsci the Party had to become the 'Modern Prince', treating politics as a science, capable of embodying the most advanced aspirations suitable to a historical epoch, and in general presenting strategy and tactics only in the context of a global picture of a future civilized order in which the working class would lead society towards communism.[26] In another metaphor Gramsci speaks of the 'State-Party'[27] to pinpoint the unity of force and consent at its core.

We finish by indicating how these rather florid allegories are concretized in a political organism which might be called the Gramscian Party, both to emphasize continuity with Leninism, and at the same time to show how many of the contradictions inherent in Lenin's conception are resolved, without, as previous 'alternatives' had done, succumbing to spontaneism.

Party and mass movement

First of all, Gramsci's Party is *necessary*, since it has a specific role. It is at the centre of developing a global alternative to present-day society, and co-ordinating all the disparate elements of revolt in a synthesis which invests every particular, immediate, localized struggle with universal importance, in the sense of bringing it into the context of other struggles and of the whole strategic movement. To argue that, in a strategy which envisages politics much more broadly than 'classical Leninism', an organizing centre is superfluous, is to fall victim to that kind of spontaneism which thinks that a general staff is only necessary for individual battles, and can be dispensed with in peacetime.

Then, it is *still* a vanguard party, but in a different sense from Lenin's. Its front-ranking position lies not so much in its ability to select the critical weakness, the decisive point at which the barricades will be breached, as in its knowledge of the way to generalize the struggle, of how the present exigencies take a place in the total scheme. The Party is thus realist and prophet rolled into one. Due to the breadth of political intervention, the élite conception disappears, since expertise is diffused amongst a far wider circle. The Party no longer lays claim to exclusive rights of leadership in all cases, even if it alone possesses the highest degree of theoretical unity. Its unity, however, is more than a bringing together of experts in various fields of struggle, for each of its particular objectives is overdetermined by the overall theoretical perspective of revolutionary transition, which encourages the participation of all leading cadres in situating each single struggle in a global context.

Nevertheless, that is not to deny that inside the Party there remain leaders and led; Gramsci's discussion in the *Notebooks* starts with precisely the recognition of this fact.[28] Significantly, though, he contrasts the desired *leadership* with the kind of administrative *control* practised by Bordiga. Leaders must deserve their authority by means of the fullest flowering of debate within the Party, ensuring that militants are loyal by conviction rather than duty. For this to happen, inner-party democracy and education are preconditions, including the provision of adequate channels for the expression of dissenting viewpoints and competing analyses, with the express possibility that they might triumph over and modify the 'official' position. Naturally, an apparatus of internal democracy that is merely an escape valve for protest is pointless from the above viewpoint. That centralism which is vital if the Party is to retain its muscle and credibility must be aimed at organizing the practical activity of cadres who represent the Party, rather than being used as an excuse for the stifling of debate and artificial denial of unrest.

Gramsci refers in particular to the existence of three 'layers' within the Party. Inevitably there will be the relatively small body of leaders at the head of the Party who are more conscious of the entire strategy and more competent public figures. It is also inevitable that there be a 'mass element' who submit to the Party's organizational influence and thereby become a substantial force. The third, intermediate, element is the 'Party cadre force' who maintain organizational, moral and intellectual contact between the leadership and the mass, and ensure that the special political abilities of the top ranks are enriched and turned to good account by the particular experiences and skills of the mass. It is clear that we have here the germ of Togliatti's post-war 'mass party',[29] a conception which has underlined the practice of the Italian Communist Party since its reconstruction in 1945, and which implicitly informs the politics of most contemporary Western European parties.

The major new problem which arises is what role the 'passive membership' play in order that they be distinguished from 'sympathizers'. This was, of course, the burning question which provoked the original split in the old Russian Party, the R.S.D.L.P.,[30] and is no less relevant today. The 'mass' Party cannot surely be defined in purely *numerical* terms, since there is also a *quality*, a qualification for membership required of even the most inactive of comrades. For example, it is reasonable to expect from every member a minimal commitment of remaining informed of Party policy through the press and publications, attending Party meetings with a certain regularity, and participating in some of the more menial aspects of Party life, even if the member does not direct the whole, or even the major part, of his or her attention towards the Party.

The crucial question remains of what relations the Party should bear to the *non-party* masses. Neither a relapse into spontaneism nor a pedagogic attitude can bridge the gap; the Party must present its position in such a way that the people recognize the way forward as relevant to their experience. Politics is very much the art of choosing between *feasible* alternatives, guiding along paths which look as if they lead somewhere. It is bad political leadership (if it can be called leadership) which rejects any concern with existing issues as reformist, or which only poses realistic alternatives in order to spring the maximum programme upon innocent followers.

The whole Gramscian strategy is very much concerned with building the widest possible mass movement, with using all possible avenues for contact with the people, with discerning the progressive potential in all expressions of rebellion and dissent. The Party has, therefore, a special 'universal' contribution to make without demanding exclusive leadership, without 'taking over' autonomous mass movements and treating them as Party 'fronts'. Take, for example, the women's movement, in which the role of Party members is to recommend which attitudes to adopt on certain questions,[31] which tactics to follow in special cases, which strategy to pursue overall, and so on; it would be fatal (and profoundly unrealistic) to try to restrict the women's movement to the expression of a sectarian viewpoint, or to insist that the Party always knows best (it doesn't – it couldn't!). The existence of non-party 'political' mass organizations is vital both before and during the revolutionary transition, to provide the broadest possible basis for mobilization and for education, and to act as a basis for a State structure founded on principles of socialist democracy.

We finish by quoting Gramsci on the complexity of the Party's relation to the broad movement; his commentary on the kind of bond which should have existed between the Ordinivisti[32] and the occupying workers is beautifully balanced, even if the actual situation in 1919 was not as he described it.

The leadership was not 'abstract'; it neither consisted in mechanically repeating scientific or theoretical formulae, nor did it confuse politics, real action, with theoretical disquisition. It applied itself to real men, formed in specific historical relations, with specific feelings, outlooks, fragmentary conceptions of the world, etc., which were the result of 'spontaneous' combinations of a given situation of material production with the 'fortuitous' agglomeration within it of disparate social elements. This element of 'spontaneity' was not neglected and even less despised. It was *educated*, directed, purged of extraneous contaminations; the aim was to bring it into line with (Marxism)[33] – but in a living and historically effective manner. The leaders themselves spoke of the 'spontaneity' of the movement, and rightly so. This assertion was a stimulus, a tonic, an element of unification in depth; above all, it denied that the movement was arbitrary, a cooked-up venture, and stressed its historical necessity. It gave the masses a 'theoretical' consciousness of being creators of *historical* and institutional *values*, of being founders of a state. This unity between 'spontaneity' and 'conscious leadership' or 'discipline' is precisely the real political action of the subaltern classes, in so far as this is mass politics and not merely an adventure by groups claiming to represent the masses.[34]

In this fine passage, in which nearly all Gramsci's themes appear, his thought completes a circle, as the vigorous intensity of his Turin experience slots into a mature perspective. His 'mass Party' cannot be reduced to either insurrectionist or social-democratic terms. Its role as leader was only feasible when it was fused with the spontaneous action of the masses. And the spontaneous action of the masses only took on a meaning when it was organically linked to the practice of a vanguard Party. At least in theory, the Jacobin limitations of Leninism had been transcended.

For us, the task is practical.

NOTES

1. Letter of 30 December 1929, in *Prison Letters*, trans. Hamish Hamilton, *New Edinburgh Review*, Gramsci Issue One.
2. See 'What is to be done?', Lenin, *Collected Works*, Vol. 5.
3. The phrase is Louis Althusser's. It is aimed against the misconception of ideology as 'false consciousness' (as in Lukács) and against crude conspiracy theories of history, which explain everything in terms of plots and ruses directed by members of the ruling class. Marx's notion of 'ideology' is completely *objective*, and derives from the practice of classes in struggle. For a rather 'advanced' explanation of

ideology, see P. Q. Hirst, *Problems in the Marxist Theory of Ideology*, published by Cambridge University CP, 1976.

Ironically, Gramsci's explicitly theoretical writing on history betrays a class-subjectivist view of Marxism, which reduces all conceptions of the world – both scientific and ideological – to historical stages of class consciousness. The fact that this does not lead Gramsci to a conspiracy theory or to a denigration of anti-spontaneist theoretical work is proof of his great political realism. For a rather slight critique of Gramsci's historicism, see Poulantzas, *Political Power and Social Classes*, NLB, 1973.

4. See, for example, P. Kropotkin, *Modern Science and Anarchism*.

5. The term 'economists' is used in its technical Marxist sense for describing a theoretical tendency that sees the economic level in society as the sole motor of history, and which expresses itself in a political practice which denigrates any agitation which does not refer directly to economic struggle. See 'What is to be done?' for Lenin's discussion. (I use the term 'social-democractic in the same paragraph in its *modern* sense, rather than in the way Lenin used it.)

6. The 'April Theses' (in Lenin: *Collected Works*, Vol. 24) provided theoretical justification for the Bolshevik strategy in 1917, especially for the concept of 'jumping stages'.

7. See D. Purdy, *Soviet Union – State Capitalist or Socialist*, CPGB, 1976.

8. This is evidenced by the failure of the campaign 'to revitalize the Soviets'; see E. H. Carr, *Socialism in One Country*, Vol. 2, Pelican, 1970.

9. R. Luxemburg, *Centralism and Democracy*.

10. Marx's reproduction schemas appear in *Capital*, Vol. 2. They explain the way in which resources are reproduced and distributed amongst the various departments of production in the labour process.

11. R. Luxemburg, *The Russian Revolution*, Ann Arbor, 1961.

12. A. Pannekoek, *Lenin as Philosopher* – published by Merlin Press, 1976, with P. Mattick's essay on Pannekoek in an appendix.

13. A. Gramsci, 'The Revolution against "Capital" ', in *Political Writings* (1910–1920), ed. Q. Hoare, Lawrence and Wishart, 1977.

14. For a discussion of this period, see G. Williams, *Proletarian Order*, Pluto, 1976, and also Q. Hoare's introduction to the *Prison Notebooks*, Lawrence & Wishart, 1971.

15. See Hoare's introduction for a picture of the PSI.

16. Gramsci, *Prison Notebooks*, p. 268.

17. Such an interpretation permeates C. Boggs, *Gramsci's Marxism*, Pluto, 1976, but the book has other redeeming features.

18. This is Poulantzas' (op. cit.) version of Gramsci's concept. It seems, reading his book, that Gramsci has been strained so finely through the Althusserian filter to remove all traces of historicism that little remains! A less critical discussion of hegemony and the State is to be found in H. Portelli, *Gramsci e il Blocco Storico*, in *Tempi Nuovi*, Laterza, Bari, 1976.

19. See Althusser's essay 'Ideology and ideological state apparatuses', in *Lenin and Philosophy*, NLB, 1971.

20. A readable presentation of this is in M. Jacques, 'Notes on the Concept of Intellectuals', *Marxism Today*, October 1971.

21. *Prison Notebooks*, p. 238.

22. *Prison Notebooks*, *passim*; for example, pp. 263, 357.

23. One could contrast this with the ideological struggle amongst the peasantry carried out by the Chinese Communist Party in the years of agrarian reform (see W. Hinton; *Fanshen*, Pelican, 1972), or during the cultural revolution.
24. *Prison Notebooks*, pp. 233–9. This strategy is implicit in the present PCI strategy, even if it is presented somewhat woollily in, for example, E. Berlinguer, *La Proposta Comunista*, Torino 1975.
25. This point must be borne in mind when analysing the defeat of the Popular Unity forces in Chile in 1973, in particular as an antidote to the 'easy excuse' of 'external forces' – be they US imperialism or the army – defeating the revolution. The UP had already lost politically *before* 11 September.
26. Naturally we do not concur with Blackburn's feeble comments in 'The Politics of Marx and Engels', NLR, 97, which suggest that Gramsci thought that Marx merely developed Machiavelli. Only doctrinaire Trotskyism could be so blind to Gramsci's real originality!
27. See Portelli, op. cit., p. 37.
28. *Prison Notebooks*, p. 144.
29. See Togliatti, *Partito nuovo*, Rinascita, 1944, and other essays in *Il Partito*, PCI, 1973. Togliatti's writings on Gramsci are collected in P. Togliatti, *Antonio Gramsci*, Roma.
30. For the history and politics of the Menshevik/Bolshevik split, see Lenin, 'One Step Forward, Two Steps Back', in *Collected Works*, Vol. 7.
31. An example is the 'Wages for Housework' campaign, which the left has consistently argued against as it reinforces sexist notions of the division of labour in the home. See M. Davis, *Link*, Spring 76.
32. The Ordinivisti were the group around *L'Ordine Nuovo*, the journal edited in Turin by Gramsci, Togliatti, Terracini and Tasca. The principal concern was the factory councils and their relations to the new state power.
33. The text reads 'Modern Theory'.
34. *Prison Notebooks*, p. 198.